ADJUST YOUR ATTITUDE

AND

LAUGH 'TIL THE COWS COME HOME!

A HELPFUL HANDBOOK OF HINTS FOR THE HUMORALLY CHALLENGED

BY LINDA HENLEY-SMITH

Adjust Your Attitude and Laugh 'Til the Cows Come Home!
A Helpful Handbook of Hints for the Humorally Challenged.

Copyright © 1997 Linda Henley-Smith

ISBN: 0-929526-80-54

Limits of Liability and Disclaimer
The author of this book has used his best efforts in its preparation. The author makes no warranty of any kind, expressed or implied, with regard to the suggestions contained herein.

The author shall not be liable in the event of incidental or consequential damages in connection with, or arising out of, the use of instructions.

Double B Publishing
4123 N. Longview
Phoenix, AZ 85014
Phone: 602-274-7236
Fax: 602-996-6928

Typesetting/Layout By:
Running Changes
1307 E. Oregon Avenue
Phoenix, AZ 85014
Phone: 602-285-1834

Illustrated in Part by Julie L. Paysnoe
Edited in Part by Lisa M. Phillips

Adjust Your Attitude and Laugh 'Til the Cows Come Home

I believe in the power of laughter. I like to laugh; it feels good and it's better exercise than frowning. Not letting laughter out causes a condition known as "humorrhoids," which can result in terminal seriousness.

I once had a rather gloomy woman snap at me when I was extolling the virtues of a good belly laugh. She said, "You can laugh 'til the cows come home but it won't change anything!"

She might be right…on one hand, laughter won't necessarily prevent bad things from happening or solve every problem. But if we condition ourselves with laughter and positive attitude, we just might have a better chance of surviving when the hard times attack us. Besides, I have learned that there is no glory in being grumpy and looking miserable…it doesn't impress anyone and it makes my face hurt.

I like the fact that we all have the choice to make our life either laffenated or delaffenated. In honor of this belief, and in memory of my aforementioned critic who chose to wear the cloak of despair…I have called this book *"Adjust Your Attitude and Laugh 'Til the Cows Come Home."*

I intend to laugh 'til the cows come home, and when they arrive, I'll invite them in and we'll all sit around and tell funny stories. Maybe they'll laugh so hard that milk will squirt out of their noses. That would be really funny.

TABLE OF CONTENTS

Introduction

Life is full of pressure. If you don't laugh, the pressure builds up, implodes, and spreads to your hips. Hopefully, in this book, you will find many reasons to laugh and incorporate humor into your life. But just in case you don't, the "hip" thing is reason enough to consider making laughter a part of your daily routine.

This book is designed to offer you a different way of thinking about humor. Perhaps you will be able to select a few humor tools to help you stay loose in times of turmoil and stress. I hope so, because that's the point!

We have all received a life. It may or may not be what we would have requested, if consulted before its onset; but nevertheless, it is ours, so we must make the best of it. Early on, we learn that practically everything in our life is beyond our control. I am reminded of this every time I try to make my hair look like something other than a used cotton swab. While we cannot always control the variables in our life, we do have the ability to control how we will react to them. Every moment of every day is a choice. We can choose to react in a positive way or we can choose to behave by becoming angry, frustrated, hurt, frightened, defeated, or hateful. But enough about me...

Our life comes with no guarantees. Sometimes things are good, and sometimes they are difficult. In other words, sometimes we get to be the bird and other times we have to be the windshield; if you get the picture.

When we received our life, we were also issued a shield of armor to help us defend ourselves against the slings and arrows of adversity. This armor is called LAUGHTER and it is an amazing thing. It never loses its effectiveness and it never wears out, no matter how often it is used. It seems to magically repair itself between uses so that each time we bring it out, it is just as good as new. No... it is better every time, because it improves with use. It just keeps getting better and better. I suppose there are four things that improve with age...laughter, fine wine, cheese, and Mel Gibson.

Laughter is many different things and takes on many different forms, which is why it is such an effective shield. It can be noisy, squeaky, snorty, high pitched, or wheezy, and can even cause your face to look funny. It can also be part of a larger force, often called a sense of humor. This not only encompasses laughter, but also includes positive attitude and a willingness to accept the world as a laugh laboratory.

I believe that humor comes from God and I am certain that God has a sense of humor. This is why my hair has a natural tendency to stick out in spikes, causing me to resemble a deranged woodpecker.

Why do I believe that I am qualified to write this book? Because I am a world class worrier, a travel agent for guilt trips, and I have an uncanny ability to find the worst in any given situation. I am Pollyanna's worst nightmare. If I can find humor in the world…anybody can!

Lesson One: Laughter and Choice

Every day, every moment, and every thought is a choice. We may choose to be controlled by fear, anxiety, anger, worry, or any other form of negativity, or we may choose to access joy in adversity.

Laughter won't guarantee that we'll always get our way, but it sure makes it a lot easier to deal with whatever happens. For instance, I once lost my job due to downsizing. Until that time, I had only thought of "downsizing" in the context of weight loss.

Anyway, I pouted, cried, moaned and groaned; caught up in my misfortune. Actually, I was quite dramatic about it, confident that everyone was dutifully sorrowful and sympathetic to my plight.

A very good friend listened to my ranting for about a week. She then said something I will never forget. She told me that no matter how I wailed and pitied myself I was still out of a job. She suggested that perhaps I might as well smile and at least try to be positive, because certainly, no one would hire me in my present state of mind.

Suddenly, it all made sense. I could be out of a job and be negative, or I could be out of a job and be positive. When I made the decision to choose to seek joy, I took a giant step toward solving the problem.

My problem and I would imagine that of many others, seemed to be that I had trouble allowing myself to accept feeling good. Somewhere along the line, I had decided that I don't deserve to feel peaceful. Nuts to that! We all deserve to choose happiness and it is ours for the taking.

The next few pages contain some humor tools to help you prepare yourself for accepting good things into your life… a quiz to help you measure your humor quotient, the all important and solemn "Humor Creed," to be memorized, recited and lived daily, and the Ten Commandments of Humor (not written by the Hand of God, but inspired by the original Ten).

"A human being will be just about as happy as he makes up his mind to be."–Abraham Lincoln
"No, I'm not happy. But I'm not unhappy about it."—Alan Bennett

---

and Laugh 'til the Cows Come Home!

TEST YOUR HUMOR QUOTIENT

	Yes	No
• I initiate fun.	☐	☐
• I try to think of ways to make work fun.	☐	☐
• I enjoy learning new fun skills.	☐	☐
• I try to expand my sense of humor.	☐	☐
• I send humorous notes and cards to friends.	☐	☐
• I am comfortable laughing out loud.	☐	☐
• I participate in "mouth aerobics" (smiling) at least once per hour.	☐	☐
• I have a "toy box" full of humor props, (magic tricks, joke books, wind-up toys, etc.)	☐	☐
• I awaken each morning with a positive attitude for the day.	☐	☐
• I try to turn negatives into positives.	☐	☐
• I keep a humor diary of funny experiences and stories.	☐	☐
• I can laugh at myself.	☐	☐

Score 1 point for each "yes" answer. If you don't register in the shaded area of the mirth-o-meter…you need to LIGHTEN UP!

HUMOR CREED

I solemly (but not too seriously) promise to give up my position as a world class worrier. I will, from this day forward, refuse to wade and wallow in the wastewater of worldly woe…choosing instead to participate in mouth aerobics (smiling) at least once every hour. I, furthermore, give myself permission to be imperfect and promise to play a little each day. In addition, I acknowledge that my mother was right…If I frown and make ugly faces, my face will freeze that way forever!

Adjust Your Attitude

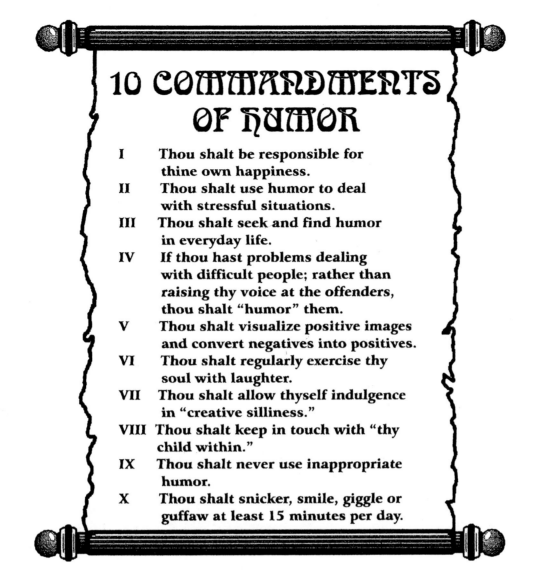

10 COMMANDMENTS OF HUMOR

I   Thou shalt be responsible for thine own happiness.

II   Thou shalt use humor to deal with stressful situations.

III Thou shalt seek and find humor in everyday life.

IV   If thou hast problems dealing with difficult people; rather than raising thy voice at the offenders, thou shalt "humor" them.

V   Thou shalt visualize positive images and convert negatives into positives.

VI   Thou shalt regularly exercise thy soul with laughter.

VII Thou shalt allow thyself indulgence in "creative silliness."

VIII Thou shalt keep in touch with "thy child within."

IX   Thou shalt never use inappropriate humor.

X   Thou shalt snicker, smile, giggle or guffaw at least 15 minutes per day.

You've Got A Choice, Joyce...
Make A New Plan, Stan

One of life's great truths seems to be that we always tend to gravitate toward what we most often think about. In other words, if we are always thinking negative thoughts, we will constantly find ourselves in negative situations, but if we move our minds away from the negative and try to focus on positive, hopeful thoughts; pretty soon, we are likely to find that those thoughts are becoming realities.

We are our thoughts. That's a pretty scary thought in itself! Our minds form pictures when we conjure up ideas. Everybody knows that the minute someone tells us not to think about something...for instance, a big purple hippo wearing ballet shoes and a tutu; that is the first and only image that will pop into our heads.

When we fill our heads with a negative thought, for example..."I just know I'm going to blow that job interview!"...that thought is imprinted on our brain; goes to work on our subconscious and shows up in our actions. The result will likely be an unsuccessful interview. We have programmed ourselves for failure and we respond in like kind.

These are not just empty words; medical studies have proven them to be valid. CAT scans of working brains have shown that our thoughts have a kind of fingerprint; rather like a neuro-signature. Repetitive thoughts cause impulses to continually retrace certain neural paths. In other words, the more we think a particular thought; the more indelibly its signature is imprinted.

Think about what you do when you're trying to memorize a phone number, a poem, or a song. You continually think of it and repeat the information until it becomes second nature. We memorize negative thoughts in the same way.

Successful people implant themselves with positive thoughts and images. I have a friend who almost always gets the job, lands the lead in the play, wins the guy...anything and everything for which she tries. When I pinned her down and demanded her secret, this is what she said: "When I am facing a challenge, I picture, in great detail, every aspect of my success in that given situation. I see myself succeeding and imagine my feelings of satisfaction and pride when I walk away with the prize. Sometimes, I even act out the scenario, writing an imaginary script for the event. I simply do not allow myself to entertain any mental pictures of negativity or failure. I do not make defeat an option."

This principle of "imaging" explains why you can wear an old, ratty tee-shirt and never spill a thing on it, because you don't care. But put on a new, white one, before going out for a spaghetti dinner, and you'll probably have the thought, "I hope I don't drool spaghetti sauce all over the front of my new shirt." Guess what will more than likely happen...you'll end up wearing half of your dinner!

Another example is the person who, when around someone with a cold, just knows for sure that he is going to catch it...he can just visualize those nasty little germs making a bee-line for his nose! Sure enough...he expects to get sick; waits for it; dreads it, and ultimately reaps his reward! His subconscious accepts sickness patterns and he becomes more vulnerable to ill health.

We all know people who seem to be "accident prone" or have a dark cloud hanging over them, and then there are those who just seem to fall into the "lucky" situations. After years of complaining that I was cursed by the troll of trouble, while others that I knew must have been born under a lucky star, it finally occurred to me that I was setting myself up for failure…I was dressing for distress and living my life by my own self-written "horror"-scope. I expected that everyone else would suck the juice out of life and leave me with the seeds. This is how I saw myself and how others saw me…until I realized that by dwelling on my fears, I was attracting what I did not want.

If we acknowledge that we can create programs in our subconscious, we will recognize the value of watching how we think! Just as we can create negativity and illness, we can also create success, confidence, and good health. We can plant the seeds of our future in dry, cracked, nutritionless dirt of negativity and despair or we can sow our seeds in the rich, fertile soil of positive thinking.

This is nothing new. Most successful people have been using the "mind magnet" theory for years! Basically, we attract what we hold in our minds. Authors from all different places and belief systems write about the mind's amazing power to attract circumstances and other people.

In "The Magic of Believing," Claude Bristol says, "Our fear thoughts are just as creative or just as magnetic in attracting troubles to us as the constructive and positive thoughts in attracting positive results." He also writes, "What may appear as coincidences are not coincidences at all but simply the working out of the pattern which you started with your own weaving."

Shakti Gawain, author of "Creative Visualization" writes, "Thought and feelings have their own magnetic energy which attracts energy of a similar nature… This is the principle which suggests that whatever you put out into the universe will be reflected back to you. What this means from a practical standpoint is that we always attract into our lives whatever we think about most, believe in most strongly, expect on the deepest levels, and/or imagine most vividly."

Our thoughts are energy and our minds are magnets. We are what we think we are. Those who picture themselves as worthwhile individuals, deserving of respect and success, will reflect this image and attract these things. They walk, talk, think, and expect happiness and fulfillment and develop a subconscious belief that these things will come to pass. These people usually reap results, which are consistent with their "inner programming."

Of course this is not to suggest that we need only to envision something for it to happen (like the band in "The Music Man," who learned to play their instruments using the "think system.") Rather, conditioning our minds with positive attitude and expectations will enable us to achieve our goals more easily than we otherwise would be able to.

We are all responsible for our own expectations. Even if someone else has told us that we are not worthy of success and happiness, we don't have to believe them, because we know better! Expect success. Expect happiness. Expect good health. Expect respect. Don't focus on what you fear, concentrate on what you want; if you want to be happy—BE HAPPY!! And remember that a positive attitude may not get you everything you want but it sure can't hurt!!!

"We magnetize into our lives whatever we hold in our thoughts." –Richard Bach

A Little Craziness Once In A While Prevents Permanent Brain Damage

An athlete would not think of starting a workout without first warming up to prevent muscle injury. An opera singer would not dream of stepping out onto a stage to perform an aria without first vocalizing and warming up his or her voice, because to do so would be dangerous to the vocal chords.

Most of us realize and appreciate the importance of conditioning our muscles, voices, skin, hair; all the parts of us…except we often overlook a very critical area. We sometimes forget to condition our attitudes. We'll take great precautions to prepare our physical self to endure stress, but we leave our emotional self out in the cold, forcing it to deal with challenges without first "warming up."

We live in the world, so we are going to experience some measure of problems. If we live our lives day in and day out in a negative state of mind, we will have no energy to face troubles when they arise. When we surround ourselves with negativity and crumple under daily stresses, we are left to face the really monumental crises with no ammunition. If our nerves are on edge and our emotions are out of balance, we have nothing to fall back on in times of genuine trouble. We need to keep our emotional reservoirs full of positive attitude and laughter to carry us through.

It's all a matter of conditioning. We can train ourselves to look for the "bad stuff" as if there were a reward for finding it, or we can condition ourselves with positive attitude and humor and refuse to "sweat the small stuff." By doing this, we are putting things into proper perspective and prioritizing our worries. If we don't waste time fretting about petty annoyances and things over which we have no control, we will be energized and ready to deal with situations of importance.

If we practice conditioning ourselves with humor, we will be emotionally in balance and able to more effectively cope with whatever comes along. Laughter won't always make everything alright, but it will create an alternative to despair. Although it is not healthy to totally deny any of our feelings, even the negative ones, it is imperative that we learn to recognize our emotions and then deal with them. We do not need to hang on to any negative thoughts for one instant longer than it takes to recognize and negate them.

An important thing to remember is that we are bigger than our problems. When something is bothering me, I am Linda with a problem...not a problem with Linda attached!

As Kurt Vonnegut said, "Laughter and tears are both responses to frustration and exhaustion. I, myself, prefer to laugh since there is less cleaning up to do afterward."

Make Humor a Habit
LAUGHTER

Lengthens your life.

Adds life to your days.

Uplifts and unifies.

Generates growth.

Heightens health.

Tickles your funny bone.

Enriches, energizes, empowers!

Relaxes and rejuvenates.

Lesson Two: Laughter and Health

In order to successfully function in this world, we must have our "wit" together. That means we have to be able to use humor to put things into proper balance and not go to pieces when life doesn't go our way.

Total health is more than our physical condition; it is more than just the absence of illness. Total health encompasses our emotional and spiritual states as well. Our sense of humor is our connection into universal wellness.

Daily stresses, left unchecked, may lead to physical illness. The best way to relieve that stress is to tap into our humor reservoir and make a conscious effort to create a positive environment. After all, if we don't take care of our body, where will our emotions live?

"Healing is simply attempting to do more of those things that bring joy into your life."– O. Carl Simonton

---

"The art of medicine consists of amusing the patient while nature cures the disease."– Voltaire

---

"I don't do anything that's bad for me. I don't like to be made nervous or angry. Any time you get upset, it tears down your nervous system."– Mae West

Laughter: A Prescription For Life

We have all heard that laughter is the best medicine, and I believe that truer words were never spoken. Apparently, I am in good company, because many people, far wiser than I, have professed this theory for years.

Nearly every culture, past and present, has incorporated humor into its healing rituals. For instance, a trip to the House of Comedy was part of the healing process in Ancient Greece, and many Native American tribes use "clown doctors" in treatment of disease. Proverbs abound, from every country, praising the virtues and values of laughter.

It is becoming more common for doctors to utilize humor in teaching patients to deal with pain and illness. One physical therapist I know teaches his patients to juggle and perform magic tricks to help take their minds off of their pain. Nursing homes are incorporating humor programs into their activity agendas, in order to help residents cope with their new environment. Laughter and a sense of humor can help us to deal with adverse situations; both physical and emotional.

Stress is the disease of the nineties. Some of us feel it; some of us are carriers! But all of us are infected or affected, in some way, by this condition. Actually, stress is not an event; it is a way in which we react to a situation.

In the midst of all the challenges with which we are faced in today's world, we often overlook the one life preserver that is always available to us in the sea of stress...a sense of humor! It is the "sixth sense" with which we've all been blessed, but we sometimes forget to use it. Many times it just seems easier to "wade and wallow in the wastewater of worldly woe."

We all carry within us the antidote to the "stress syndrome." This anti-toxin is our ability to laugh and it's one of the most powerful medicines around! Laughter is the great communicator and the great equalizer. It allows us to take a break from negative situations and stand back to gain proper perspective. Laughter is "mental floss" to clear our minds; exercise for our souls.

We are never going to escape stress. We can run, but we cannot hide! The truly healthy people are not those who have less stress, but rather, the ones who have learned to deal with it effectively, using humor skills and attitude adjustment techniques. We can either "lighten up" and thrive or "tighten up" and dive!

Many businesses encourage their employees to join health clubs and keep themselves physically fit; which is certainly important. On the other hand, how many organizations take as much interest in the mental condition of their members? Taking a vacation once a year is not enough to insure solid emotional health...people need to "pump up" their funny bones on a regular basis.

You may not be aware of this, but an adult's minimum daily requirement of Vitamin H (for Humor) is fifteen good laughs a day. I'm sure that many of us are backlogged in this area.

Now, I have reached the conclusion that my fat cells shall always be with me, but my brain cells may come and go. I do not choose to rent my brain to negative thoughts. Every moment spent on a negative thought is time away from a positive one. So, I have elected to embark on a rigorous workout routine of "LAFFERCISE."

A good belly laugh is healthy…it releases endorphins (natural "uppers") and opiates (natural pain killers) into our systems, increases heart rate and circulation and exercises virtually every internal organ. A rousing twenty-second guffaw is equal to a three-minute aerobic workout on a rowing machine. Yippee! I've waited a long time for a way to exercise without having to wear those tiny little spandex shorts which make me look like a stuffed sausage. Imagine the existence of exercise gurus with fluffy bodies and big grins, counting out "mouth lifts," instead of stomach crunches!

In my Humor Workshops, I sometimes offer some examples of laffercise routines, designed to assist the "humorally challenged." Some people have become so rigid, they look like they would just disintegrate on the spot if made to do anything even remotely silly. I honestly believe, however, there is hope for even the most terminally solemn.

Laffercise is a series of physical movements, which are designed to condition your mind with the liberating power of silliness. If you make silly noises, goofy faces and odd gestures; in other words, look foolish, and find that you not only survive, but also actually feel better, you begin to realize that you will not lose your professionalism if you play a little bit. I get a kick out of watching people enter into these workshops with that glazed look of seriousness and seeing them leave blowing the party noisemakers that we hand out. Some of these workshop participants have taken great strides in risk taking, by simply making contact with that child within them.

Hearty laughter helps to ease muscle tension and it breaks spasm and pain cycles, which are often seen in rheumatoid diseases. Most of our muscles become nearly flaccid when we belly laugh. I realize that this could become ugly, but it IS healthy.

When we participate in Laffercise, we are showing the world that we care enough about ourselves to treat ourselves nicely. We are also "adding more days to our life by adding more life to our days!"

NAME:_____ DATE:_____
ADDRESS:_____

Vitamin H –
15 Laughs Per Day

REMARKS:
EXP. DATE   *No expiration.*

Rx: Humor...

The Medicine with No Bad Side Effects

15 good laughs per day provide the minimum daily requirement of Vitamin H (for humor).

"A merry heart doeth good like a medicine; but a broken spirit drieth the bones."–Proverbs 17:22

LAUGHTER...

☺ Exercises the cardiovascular system

☺ Releases endorphins (nature's uppers)

☺ Stimulates practically all of the large internal organs

☺ Improves posture and appearance

☺ Relaxes muscles and drains tension

☺ Releases opiates (natural painkillers) into the bloodstream

☺ Is great aerobic exercise...
(20 seconds of guffawing equals 3 minutes on a rowing machine)

Laughter is to the soul what exercise is to the body.

A Portrait Of Panic

There are many things, which cause the average human to feel stress, embarrassment or downright panic. Recently, when my "coiffure enhancement" (that's hairpiece to you and me) took off on its own and left my head, choosing instead to fly into the audience during my presentation which was being televised, I experienced all three of the aforementioned emotions.

I felt all of the universal symptoms of fear…adrenaline rushing, heart pumping, face flushing, and the interesting combination of wanting to run while feeling like my feet were nailed to the floor. The way we react to psychological danger (like being embarrassed in front of masses of people) and our response to physical danger result in similar bodily symptoms. An endocrinologist by the name of Hans Selye, was a pioneer in psychosomatic medicine, which began to recognize the connection between perceived stress and bodily functions. His theory of the "general-adoption syndrome" divides our reaction to danger into three phases.

THE ALARM REACTION: As you well know, the reaction to perceived danger is the fight or flight response. It enables us to run faster, scream louder, and has even been known to allow slightly built women to lift cars off of people. In cases of physical danger, this is a great system, but the trouble is…our bodies react in the same way in cases of emotional stress.

RESISTANCE: In this stage, our brain chemistry adjusts to allow our body to develop a tolerance for the stress. It's only designed to handle it for a limited amount of time…say, long enough to run away from the physical danger. This whole fight or flight mechanism was no doubt installed by our Maker to allow us an opportunity to escape from life threatening situations. We misuse it when we keep it in "over-drive" during our emotionally stressful scenarios.

EXHAUSTION: When we keep our stress level up for extended periods of time as a result of worry, anxiety, anger or frustration, the heightened hormonal secretions lead to pathological changes in our bodies. William W. Ruch, a professor of psychology at the University of Southern California explains this as follows: "Many of the physiological dysfunctions which originally appeared during the alarm reaction begin to reappear." He goes on to say that after awhile, our organs are no longer able to adapt to the continuing stress. The end result can be emotional illness or physical disease and death.

Once we know the dangers of keeping ourselves in a heightened state of panic, how do we go about preventing it? Humor therapist, C. W. Metcalf, writes about the limbic system, which governs and manages the chemistry of our emotions. It is a delicately wired system; any extreme emotional reaction may trigger its opposite. Metcalf explains that this is why some people laugh at funerals. The point is, we cannot deny any of our emotions because if we cut ourselves off from feeling the bad, by ignoring our feelings, we are also cutting ourselves off from feeling the good. So we need to acknowledge our fears and then shift our thoughts away from them as soon as possible, by utilizing laffercise or any other attitude adjustment tools we find useful. Some of these techniques will be mentioned in the following chapters.

This is YOUR BODY
(You may add the appropriate parts.)

Adjust Your Attitude

This is **YOUR BODY** on **ANGER & STRESS**

Brain: Anxiety and depression may be triggered by stress.

Mouth: Mouth ulcers sometimes appear.

Blood Pressure: INCREASES.

Heart: disturbances of heart rhythm often occur in times of distress.

Digestive Tract: Stress contributes to irritable colon, ulcers and gastritis.

ADRENALINE FLOWS AT HIGH LEVELS.

Skin: Some people suffer rash outbreaks.

Muscles: Tighten up and twitch.

and Laugh 'til the Cows Come Home!

This is YOUR BODY on LAUGHTER

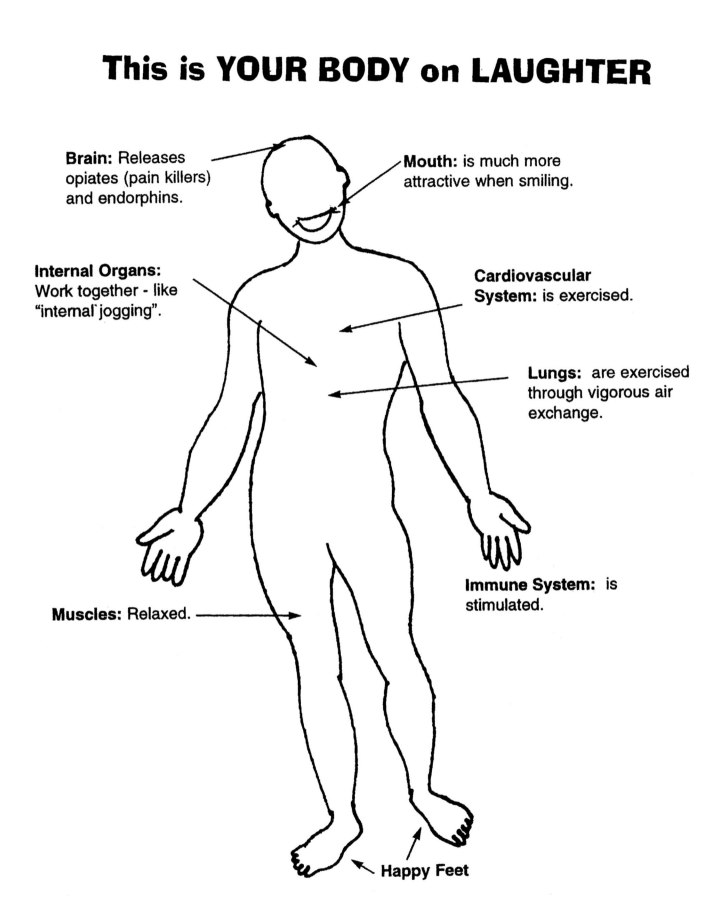

Brain: Releases opiates (pain killers) and endorphins.

Mouth: is much more attractive when smiling.

Internal Organs: Work together - like "internal jogging".

Cardiovascular System: is exercised.

Lungs: are exercised through vigorous air exchange.

Immune System: is stimulated.

Muscles: Relaxed.

Happy Feet

Laugh For the Health of It

At one time or another in our existence here on earth, it seems as if each of us becomes a caregiver. When we are young, we may start by taking care of our pets. Then we grow up and care for our spouse and children. Many of us end up caring for our parents and the list goes on and on. The problem seems to be that we often forget to take care of ourselves.

Our bodies don't come with owner's manuals and we just have to learn by trial and error. But one thing is for sure…in order to care for others, we have to begin by keeping our mind, body, and spirit healthy.

Too often, we try to do for others and neglect our own needs and then follow it up with a big dose of creative suffering. This is called martyrdom and believe me, it went out with Joan of Arc.

In his book, Anatomy of an Illness, Norman Cousins related his experiences of launching into a systematic program of laughter therapy designed to conquer his painful and potentially terminal disease.

Knowing that negative emotions produce negative chemical changes in the body, Mr. Cousins reasoned that conversely, positive emotions might just have therapeutic value and produce positive chemical changes. Deciding to exercise a measure of control over his own illness, he began to "treat" himself with laughter. Films of old comedy routines were brought into his hospital room and so began the laughter prescription.

He tells of the elation he felt when he realized that a ten-minute belly laugh resulted in two hours of pain-free sleep. When blood tests showed that his sedimentation rate dropped several points after each laugh episode, he was convinced that there is truth to the old theory that laughter is the best medicine.

Research has established the existence of substances in the brain called endorphins, with a molecular structure and effects very much like morphine. Endorphins are natural "uppers" and natural relaxants. We know now, that laughter stimulates our brain to produce an alertness hormone called catecholamine, which in turn stimulates the release of endorphins into our bloodstream.

The healing power of humor is certainly nothing new. Cultures from the beginning of time have realized the importance of laughter. But in the thirty years since Norman Cousins took charge of his own mind and body and became an active participant in his mental and physical health, doctors have done extensive research to prove the benefits of laughter to the immune system.

Dr. Lee S. Berk, of California's Loma Linda University School of Medicine measured the immune response of five men who were watching humorous videotapes of a comedian. The volunteers showed an increase in immune cell production and a decrease in the hormones that depress the immune system.

Experiments at New England College in Springfield, Massachusetts showed an elevation of salivary immunoglobulin, an immune substance that wards off respiratory illnesses, in volunteers who watched a comedy videotape. All this medical talk simply means that he who laughs...lasts! Humor is indeed the miracle drug with no bad side effects. It has amazing restorative and recuperative capabilities. We just need to learn to trust in the power of laughter in our health. As Albert Schweitzer said, "Every man carries his own doctor inside him."

Lesson Three:
Laughter and Personalities

Everyone has a sense of humor...some may forget to use it, but it's there somewhere! As a matter of fact, humor is a very important part of our personalities; and how we choose to use it can greatly affect how we get through life's little and large challenges.

Recognizing the differences in people's humor personalities can make it easier to understand why we all relate, respond and react to situations differently. Knowing this allows us to deal with negativity and potentially explosive situations.

Understanding that it is acceptable and even desirable for each of us to have our own distinct humor personalities, and keeping an open mind in dealing with other people's attitudes will make relationships sail a little more smoothly.

"If I thought that everybody else in the world thought the same way about things as I did...I'd be afraid that I had wandered into some kind of strange zone where no one had the gumption to be an individual. And, if they thought just like me... I would seriously doubt their intelligence."
–H. Thompson (retirement community resident)

"What sunshine is to flowers, smiles are to humanity. They are but trifles, to be sure; but scattered along life's pathway, the good they do is inconceivable."–Joseph Addison

---

The Many Faces Of Humor

Everyone has a sense of humor. Sometimes you will meet someone whose funnybone has been buried so deeply and for so long, you wonder if it can ever be found. And sometimes, that funnybone will be so deteriorated that it seems less than functional, but it's there, none the less.

People laugh at different things, and that's just the way it is. For instance, my husband never laughs at comedians, funny movies or jokes. He does, however, find great joy and amusement in watching me walk from the restroom, through a restaurant full of people, with the back of my skirt tucked into my pantyhose. I laugh at sit-coms; my husband laughs at me. See how it works?

Even though, at times, it causes frustration, the differences in people are what make them so special. Everybody is a piece of the puzzle and the picture is not complete without all of the pieces. It is very much like an orchestra comprised of many types of instruments, playing different notes and making different sounds. If everyone blew, thumped, banged, or clanged at will, the result would be noisy chaos. But, when playing together under the baton of a master conductor, they make beautiful music.

It is not for us to try to convince others to share our sense of humor or to laugh at the same things that we consider funny. Of course, that would be almost impossible. Humor is a conditioner. It is a way to create an atmosphere of comfort, which puts others at ease. A person who conveys a sense of humor, is sending a message that he or she is approachable and non-intimidating.

Daily, we are faced with a variety of personalities. In fact, our homes and places of business are virtual studies in personality diversity. If there are twenty-five people in a room, there are twenty-five different characters. In order to effectively communicate with all of them, we must find some common denominator. Often, that common link may be a sense of humor. Even though we may not laugh at the same things, if it is established that it is acceptable to enjoy ourselves while working, and if an atmosphere of lightheartedness permeates our environment, we create a bond and a foundation on which to build successful communication. In other words, people like to feel good. If a family member, co-worker, customer, etc., recognizes that you value fun and understand the empowerment of humor, he or she will feel less pressure to be perfect and more freedom to exercise creativity. Of course, everyone has to be aware of the bounds of appropriate humor.

Studies have shown that children who are brought up with humor and laughter have higher self-esteem, retain more of what they are taught, and exhibit more creativity than those who are subjected to humorless, rigid rules. In short, humor liberates learning, maximizes memory, and encourages creativity. If it works with kids, it will work with adults in your office.

We don't always know what's going on in another person's life. A person who is nasty and negative may be trying to cope with some private problem. The smile and kind word we give them might just be what he needs to help him along. Of course, that same person might be one of those who just enjoys being a grim reaper, in which case, it might be acceptable to bop him on the head with a cardboard tube. Just kidding. Common sense is necessary in assessing personalities and determining how people will be affected by our humor. We have to use humor sense in our sense of humor. It goes without saying that humor is never appropriate when it is directed to a particular ethnic or religious group, hurtful in any way, or offensive in nature.

No matter what an individual's humor personality may be, most of us have one thing in common…we like to feel good and we like to have a good time every once in a while. When people live or work together, they become a team. A group is merely a bunch of people, but a team is a group with a common goal. You and your family or co-workers are a team and your goal is to have a pleasant experience doing whatever you are doing. Consider that the unifying bond of your team might well be laughter. It might help…it sure can't hurt. A genuine smile (not a smirk) never offends anyone.

"In matters of humor, what is appealing to one person is appalling to another." – Melvin Helitzer

---

Your Humor Personality

I have found that there are basically four humor personality types. My research is totally unscientific and totally devoid of psychological foundation…but it's fun!

The next time you are in a large group of people, try playing a little game with yourself as you watch how different folks convey their senses of humor. Imagine that we are all members of the animal kingdom and have some fun equating people's humor styles to the traits of different critters.

For instance, there are those of us who will laugh at almost any-thing and express our glee in loud, chattery, contagious peals of laughter. We love to be the center of attention and sometimes feel uncomfortable when there is a lull in the excitement. We jump around from group to group, thoroughly enchanted with meeting new people and sharing funny stories. Most likely, everyone around us knows when we think something is funny, because we are not quiet. We are not above trying new things and are usually not afraid of appearing a bit silly. We are the MONKEYS.

Then, there are those of us who generally take things a tad more seriously. We definitely have a sense of humor, but are more selective as to our demonstration of it. We are organized and neat and quiet laughers. We, unlike the monkeys, do not necessarily feel the need to be in the middle of everything, although we are certainly social creatures and can enjoy a good laugh. We just don't like to call attention to ourselves with our laughter. We are the CATS.

We are aggressive and bold and usually like to take control of a situation. We exude confidence and although we enjoy a good laugh, we aren't often given to fits of giggling. We appreciate humor but don't really feel comfortable expressing it through silliness. We usually aren't the type to wear goofy hats, etc., so when we do, the incongruity of it all is really quite funny. We tend to take life on a "work now, play later" basis and don't like to waste a lot of time on long, drawn out laughs. We are the LIONS.

No one really ever knows exactly what we think is funny because we don't show much humor emotion. We keep our laughter hidden; we are quiet, relaxed and easy-going. We are patient and balanced and are usually very calm, cool and collected. Nothing ever seems to knock us off guard and cause us to giggle uncontrollably. We could be laughing hysterically within and allow but a mere smile to show on the outside. We drive other humor personalities crazy because we never really let go and guffaw. We are steady. We are the TORTOISES.

We all have a sense of humor, we just deal with it and demonstrate it differently. Sometimes CATS and TORTOISES who live or work together, might not understand each other's humorous treatment of a situation and a LION might easily lose patience with a MONKEY who would rather laugh than work. By recognizing people's unique humor personalities, we can learn to respect and appreciate the many different faces of humor.

There are basically
four humor personality types...

Knowing the characteristics of each can help you to understand the humor quotient of the people in your life and why they may act the way they do.

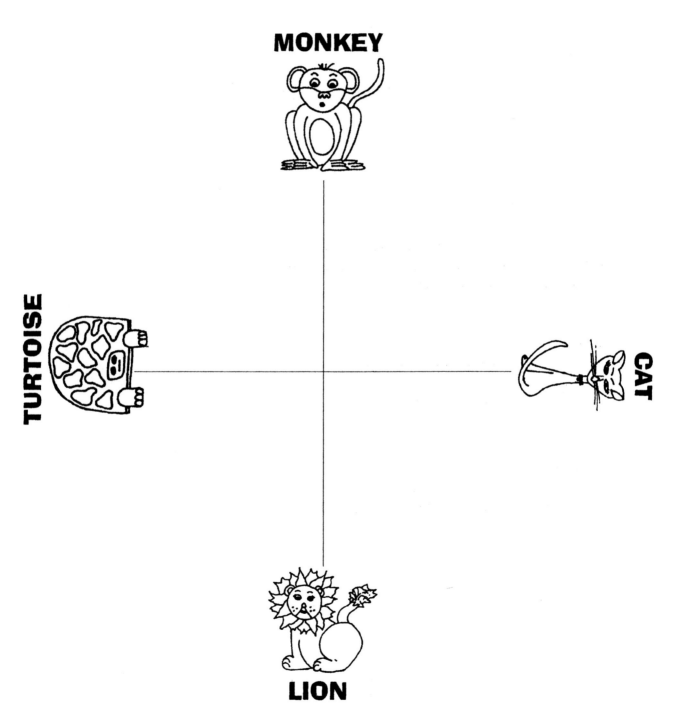

HUMOR PERSONALITY ASSESSMENT

Please answer "yes" or "no" to the following questions:

I laugh at almost anything.	Yes	No
I will talk to anyone at anytime.	Yes	No
I love to tell stories.	Yes	No
(I can make a 10 minute trip to the store into a mini-series.)		
I like to be the center of attention.	Yes	No
I keep in touch with the child within.	Yes	No

If you have at least 4 "yes" answers, you are probabaly a MONKEY humor personality. You enjoy life and can find humor in just about everything. You like to laugh - usually loudly (even if you're not sure what is funny.) You may have been described as "effervescent."

I generally take life seriously.	Yes	No
I am very organized and neat.	Yes	No
I am a list maker.	Yes	No
I do not like to be in the spotlight.	Yes	No
I am a quiet laugher.	Yes	No

If you have at least 4 "yes" answers, you are probabaly a CAT humor personality. You like structure and order; your sense of humor reflects this. Your laugh is quiet and subtle.

I am aggressive and bold.	Yes	No
I am impatient.	Yes	No
I like to take control (my way is the right way.)	Yes	No
I exude confidence.	Yes	No
My laugh is one short and loud blast.	Yes	No
(I don't waste time on giggles.)		

If you have at least 4 "yes" answers, you are probabaly a LION humor personality. You know that there is only one way to do things and that way is your way! You don't have much time to waste on long drawn out laughs; yours is a quick loud blast!

I keep emotions hidden.	Yes	No
I am quiet.	Yes	No
I am relaxed and easy-going.	Yes	No
I am patient and balanced.	Yes	No
I am usually calm, cool and collected.	Yes	No

If you have at least 4 "yes" answers, you are probabaly a TORTOISE humor personality. No one ever really knows what you're thinking - you make people nervous...you don't really ever laugh out loud, you just smile.

I'm Okay, But You're Weird

It is the human condition to take notice of other people's characteristics and compare them to our own. It seems as if we are constantly checking to see how we or they measure up. If someone doesn't laugh at the same things that we find hilarious, we often proclaim them to be lacking a sense of humor. The person who has no inhibitions about doing the "chicken dance" in a public place, cannot understand why his less liberated friend is such a "stuffed shirt!"

It has probably always been like that. I have a mental picture of Eve snorting with laughter about something the serpent said, and Adam looking at her like she had lost her marbles.

The fact is, we all come from different backgrounds and experiences, so it stands to reason that we will not all find humor in the same things. Unfortunately, some people have spent many years living with anger, fear, resentment, and other "laughter killers." An adult who was emotionally abused as a child may interpret teasing as a painful reminder of a past that filled him with self-loathing.

In his book, "Lighten Up," Humorologist, C.W. Metcalf writes of his experiences in the Twelve Step program. He says that in many treatment programs, a written inventory is used as an integral part of the recovery process. The idea is for the person to write down the resentment, anger, and fear that weakened him until addictive behavior masked those feelings. Metcalf explains that this inventory is often the turning point in helping people to regain health, self-respect, and a humor perspective. He suggests that we all should create a Humor Inventory to help us remember, recognize and rearrange reactions that have warped our humor perspectives.

For instance, as a child, you may have had an experience in which you felt ungainly and clumsy and were the butt of some unkind teasing. How did that make you feel? Probably, it made you feel isolated and left out. As a result of that, you may have grown up to equate teasing and humor as a weapon that always causes injury. Perhaps this is something that has prohibited you from taking risks, or caused you to use humor as a defense, rather than an enhancement. Once you have identified the feeling, you can decide what to do with it. Hopefully, you will choose to stop thinking of humor as a weapon and respond in a more healthy way, to those who tease you.

Another part of the Humor Inventory involves thinking about your humor role models. As a young person, were you encouraged or discouraged from using humor as a coping tool? What was your most embarrassing moment and how did you deal with it? Are any of those feelings of adolescent insecurity still hanging on?

The main function of taking our humor pulse is to cut through all the excess baggage and get right to the heart of what our sense of humor is all about. By understanding why we laugh at something or not or why we might be afraid of looking silly in front of our colleagues, we can take steps toward getting the maximum benefit from our funny bones. It will also shed some light on why others may not always be on the same humor wavelength as we are.

Sometimes, we just need to be available as Mirth Donors, ready to provide humor transfusions to those who are struggling to build up their "laugh count." And sometimes we need to let go of those old, painful insecurities and go forth into uncharted Humor Territory. We will save ourselves a lot of grief if we just accept the fact that everyone's sense of humor is a little bit different from the next person's. Case in point: Don't attempt to get out of a traffic ticket by wearing a clown nose...I tried it and the policeman was not amused.

Adjust Your Attitude

Lesson Four:
Laughter and Surviving Parenthood

In ancient times, a king decided to find and honor the greatest person among his subjects. A person of wealth and property was singled out. Another was praised for his healing powers; another for her wisdom and knowledge of the law. Still another was lauded for his business acumen. Many other successful people were brought back to the palace, and it became evident that the task of choosing the greatest would be difficult.

Finally, the last two candidates stood before the king. They were a little old woman and a little old man. They both had hair of white and wore the lines of age on their faces. Their eyes shone with the light of knowledge, understanding, and love.

"Who are these people?" asked the king.
"What worthy things have they done?"

"They are parents," answered the king's aide. The people applauded and cheered, and the king came down from his throne to honor them.–Anonymous

---

Parents impart many pearls of wisdom, but none so precious as the lessons of laughter and play.

Humor 101: The Laughing Parent

I am a parent. This means that I am also, at times, a friend, a foe, a winner, a loser, happy, depressed, joyful, worried, elated, humbled, courageous, and afraid. I am also sometimes a magician. I have been given a marvelous gift…the opportunity to watch my children as a thought takes root in their brains and develops into an exciting idea. With this, comes the joy of seeing a child I love grow into a young adult that I respect, admire, and like.

I am sometimes a teacher and sometimes a student. Each day, I learn about the joy of people helping other people and I am amazed at the power of a smile and a kind word. Raising a child is very much like planting a tree. We must gently plant the seeds in the fertile soil of security, water them from the reservoir of knowledge, and root them firmly in love. Then, we must nourish them with laughter and enthusiasm, and tend to them regularly, constantly pruning the sucker shoots of negativity, which drain energy. I read somewhere that by the time a child is eighteen years old, he has been told "NO," or "You can't do that!" over 150,000 times. A child lives what he learns.

Positive attitude is nourishment for all of us. It is "caught" not "taught." Humor creates a non-threatening environment, which allows us to feel relaxed; therefore, exchange is freer and creativity and productivity are fostered.

Unfortunately, there are those among us who still wrongly equate having a good time with goofing off. Actually, nothing could be further from the truth. Laughter liberates learning and maximizes memory. It is an integral part of the child-rearing process. If children learn to laugh at themselves through creative silliness, they won't come apart when they find themselves in stressful situations.

Humor defuses negativity. In a confrontation, unexpected uses of humor can defuse an explosive situation and put things into proper perspective. The effectiveness of humor as a communication tool is often underestimated.

Most of us have created for ourselves, numerous ways to feel miserable and only a few ways to feel truly good. I suppose this puts us in the position of not being disappointed when things don't turn out favorably.

We make our own rules as to how to react to any given situation and we determine whether we will derive pain or pleasure from the outcome. Humor serves as a way to "reframe" our problems. This term is borrowed from the world of art…changing the frame around a picture changes the way the picture looks. When a situation is reframed with humor, the facts remain the same, but the image is different.

We, as parents, have an incredible responsibility to our children. We must teach them by the moral and ethical rules in which we believe, but our responsibilities are much greater than that. We must teach them that feeling good and having a positive attitude is an asset in problem solving. We must teach that happiness is not a set of circumstances; it's a way of life and a state of mind. We must teach that techniques and steps can't lead us to success; that peace of mind, not "things" should be our goal. We must demonstrate the difference between striving for happiness and simply moving away from unhappiness. Maintaining a positive attitude will not always solve our problems, but it gives us a head start and a better chance to find healthy solutions.

Laughter is the great communicator. When dealing with diversity, humor is the shortest distance between people. If we can find something about which we can all laugh, we have found a common denominator and a starting place for a healthy relationship. If there is laughter in the present, there is hope for the future.

"When the tickly feeling inside your tummy comes out of your mouth…that's a laugh!"– Stephanie G. (Age 5½)

"Laughter is a bubbling spring deep inside one's soul, which has no choice but to escape and become part of the universe."– Melvin P. (Age 88)

"Insanity is hereditary…you get it from your kids."– Anonymous

---

Give Yourself and Your Children an Attitude of Altitude

Anyone who has spent any time living has probably learned that if you are having a life with no problems, you are not having a life!

It's important to send a clear message to children that no one ever promised life to be clear sailing. That is not the same thing as teaching them to expect the worst, but a little realism doesn't hurt. The fact is, everything doesn't always go our way.

What we want our young people to understand, is how to adjust their attitude and raise their altitude. This means that we want them to learn to view any situation that troubles them, in two different ways.

If we see a situation as a problem, we need to focus on viewing it as a challenge, instead. Believe me, there is a difference in those two viewpoints. When we see something as a problem, it becomes a barrier, whereas, if we adjust our attitude and consider it a challenge, a troublesome situation becomes a learning experience.

We have the obligation to teach our kids that they ultimately have dominion over their lives. We all have the right to do those things which are life-enhancing and uplifting. Our children must recognize that they are stronger than anything that stands in the way of them achieving their self-empowering goals. This means when peer pressure rears its head and a child is tempted to "go with the flow" to avoid rejection, he must feel that it's okay to take advantage of his options. We can help our children by arming them with the power of alternatives and choices, which will help them achieve an attitude of altitude.

Rather than to wait until a challenge occurs and then try to teach alternative choice management skills in the heat of a crisis, we should discuss and reaffirm these ideas with our children in "peace time." It is advantageous to conduct exercises, which encourage them to entertain positive decision-making thoughts to resolve conflicts. Creating hypothetical conflict-based scenarios and allowing the kids to role-play and talk through possible reactions and resolutions is one way to foster creative solution-oriented thinking. If we teach and encourage positive thinking as an alternative to violent behavior in conflict resolution, we will be helping them to condition themselves to be able to choose an attitude of altitude and avoid slipping into a habit of non-productive negativity.

Negative attitude is an addiction, just as surely as any drug. It permeates our lives and destroys hope. It is true that misery loves company. Sometimes, negative people tend to gravitate toward others who share their joy of groaning and moaning. Negativity tends to manifest itself in other addictions, which can keep us in that eternal downward spiral. A wonderful gift we can give to our children is the spirit of worthiness and empowerment...the birthright of each and every one of us! This gift is given through the consistent nurturing of habitual positive focus. A sense of humor is an important part of the process.

I learned the hard way if I was going to incorporate humor into my life, I needed to embrace the "4-A" principle. First, I needed to be **Aware** that humor is all around me and that it is there for the taking. I make choices in life and I have the ability to access joy in adversity. Secondly, I had to recognize and **Accept** that humor is an empowering force, a coping device, and a healing tool. Next, I needed to **Adopt** an attitude of altitude. Again, that means making choices, opening myself to new suggestions, and being willing to release certain negative habits and thoughts that keep me buried in my "comfortable" misery. Last, and probably the most difficult, I learned that I must constantly work toward **Application** of humor to my everyday challenges.

I have found that by following the 4-As, I am more effectively able to maintain a reasonably positive attitude. And when I have altitude...I leave all the "junk" below and soar above it. I found that with that attitude lift, I could turn my life around. I once had a woman tell me that her husband had finally turned his life around. He used to be miserable and depressed and now he's depressed and miserable! That's not quite the turnaround she had been hoping for.

Michelangelo was once asked how he could possibly create such extraordinarily beautiful pieces of art out of lumps of rock and stone. He answered by saying that the beauty and the art was already there in the stone. God created it. All he did was chip away the excess pieces to reveal the masterpiece. I think that's a great analogy to our souls. The peaceful beauty is already in there. All we need to do is chip away the excess pieces…remorse, anger, fear, guilt, and all the other negative emotions that hide our inner beauty and perfect peace.

In order to change our attitude, we must do something to lift our spirits…that's the altitude part. Positive affirmations and visualization can put us in the frame of mind that will be conducive to productive thinking. In visualization, we can use our imagination to make everything just the way we want it. There are no restrictions.

The objective is to break a negative pattern and redefine the situation. A problem has a negative connotation; a challenge suggests a positive outcome.

Negativity immobilizes us and keeps us from creating solutions. It also stands in the way of our good health. We can't afford to waste time with a negative attitude because it lowers our altitude. In other words, we can't soar with the eagles if we're grounded like the turkeys!

"Positive attitudes; optimism, high self-esteem, and out-going nature, joyousness, and the ability to cope with stress may be the most important basis for continued good health."–Helen Hayes

---

Rules Of Life

☺ Always take your work seriously and yourself lightly.

☺ Everyone needs to be responsible for his or her own happiness.

☺ Do not deny or suppress negative feelings…identify them, deal with them and then let them go.

☺ Consider all of the options. If something isn't working, try it a different way. You wouldn't stand in a darkened room and continue to flip the light switch if nothing happened when you did it. You would find another way to fill the room with light. If your life "isn't working," try another path. Learn to create alternatives.

☺ Don't live your life in the "IF ONLY" syndrome…IF ONLY I was richer, thinner, taller, smarter, more popular, etc. etc. etc…then I'd be happy! To live that way is to set yourself up for failure. Do not depend on things or situations to make you happy.

☺ Humor should always include; never exclude anyone. Always use appropriate humor; laugh at yourself, but never at others in a harmful way. Humor should build confidence, never destroy it.

☺ Laughter is the spark that ignites success. Like a boomerang, we get back what we send out. With our attitude, we make a statement about who we are, where we work and what we do. Having a sense of humor is being able to break away from habitual thinking.

☺ Sometimes it is better to simply move away from negativity rather than to constantly search for happiness.

☺ Don't believe in defeat, because every loss teaches a lesson. Believe in your potential and empower yourself with *positivity.* (That's not a word, but it should be!)

☺ Use a sense of humor and a positive attitude to write your own script and chart your own course for success.

☺ There is no such thing as a "bad" day. Unpleasant things might happen, but a day is just a day. It is up to us to determine how we are going to deal with the events of the day. When we have been given the precious gift of another day of life…how can it be bad? We can't always control the environment but we can control the way we react, how we relate to different people and how long we allow ourself to feel angry, depressed, or miserable. We may not be able to choose the way we die…but we can choose the way we live!

How To...
Cope Instead Of Mope,
Thrive Instead Of Dive
and Enjoy An Attitude Of *Altitude*

Look through the following list and put a check by the method you are already using. Now put a star by the things you'd be willing to try.

_____ I take mini-vacations from my work using touchstones, which remind me of happy times. This allows me to regain some of those joyful feelings.

_____ I visualize myself where I want to be.

_____ I accept the support of other people and I offer my support to others. If I am troubled, I try to come out of myself and help someone else.

_____ I use prayer and/or meditation to help me to connect with inner wisdom and find a sense of peace.

_____ I make time to find the elf in mysELF and play a little each day.

_____ I open my mind to new thoughts, which help me to create new feelings.

_____ I try to exercise regularly to relieve my stress and "mental floss" my brain.

_____ I find time for the hobbies which energize and refocus me.

_____ I try to surround myself with people and things that empower and encourage me.

_____ I try to exercise the "boomerang theory." Whatever you send out will come right back to you. Positivity breeds positivity. Negativity spreads like a disease.

_____ I try to limit my time as a "worry warrior."

_____ I make an effort to go and grow with the flow. Nothing is worth jeopardizing my physical and mental health.

_____ I exercise my option to feel well and be at peace.

_____ I strive to feel guiltless about taking care of myself and treating myself well.

Kids Can Either Crack You Up
or Cause You to Crack-Up

There's no doubt that parenting can be stressful, but there are also a lot of laughs to be laughed. There is not a parent around who could not make a fortune in a comedy club telling stories about his or her child. Kids are a rich source of humor and if you're not keeping a journal of funny things your kids, grandkids, students, or friend's kids say, you're missing a golden opportunity.

A teacher friend of mine keeps her journal by her bed and reads from it every night to condition her mind with humor before she goes to sleep. She has been teaching for twenty-five years, so she has quite a few stories.

The best part of "kid humor" is that most of the time, they don't know they're being funny. I'll never forget my first year of teaching kindergarten. We were discussing our middle names and learning to print them. When I asked Willie about his, he looked at me and said proudly that his middle name was Dammit. Thinking I had misunderstood, I asked him to repeat that. He patiently told me again and this time added that he was certain this was his name because every morning his mother called him for breakfast and said very clearly, "Willie Dammit, hurry up!"

Then there was the time that six-year-old Jodie was explaining to the class that her mother had said she was sorry she had ever gotten Skipper because all he did was lay around and scratch himself. Thinking that Skipper was the family dog, I made the comment that pets sometimes do things like that. Imagine my surprise when Jodie informed me that Skipper was not her pet...he was her stepfather!

Here are some gems collected from the files of teachers and parents:

The children of the Tsar are Tsardines.

Inhabitants of Paris are called Parasites.

Feminine hygiene products are America's gross national product.

In the Christian religion, a man can have only one wife. This is called monotony.

Trigonometry is when a lady marries three men at the same time.

Joseph Haydn had a lot of will power. He died in 1809 and is still dead.

Q. What would you do in the case of a person bleeding from a head wound?
A. I would tie a tourniquet tightly around his neck.

The best way to eat cream cheese and lox is with a beagle.

To collect fumes of sulfur, hold a deacon over a flame in a test tube.

Algebraic symbols are used when you don't know what you're talking about.

Robert Louis Stevenson got married and went on his honeymoon. It was then that he wrote, "My Travels With a Donkey."

The chief cause of divorce is marriage.

In many states with the death penalty, people are put to death by electrolysis.

In order to be a good nurse, you must be completely sterile.

Queen Elizabeth was the Virgin Queen. As a queen she was a success. When Elizabeth exposed herself before her troops, they all shouted "hurrah," then her navel went out and defeated the Spanish Armadillo.

Beethoven expired in 1827 and later died for this.

John Milton wrote "Paradise Lost." Then his wife died and he wrote "Paradise Regained."

The Greeks invented three kinds of columns: Corinthian, Doric and Ironic. They also had myths. A myth is a female moth.

Socrates died from an overdose of wedlock.

In Bible times, Jacob, son of Isaac, stole his brother's birthmark.

Solomon had 500 wives and 500 porcupines.

Homer wrote the Oddity, in which Penelope was the last hardship that Ulysses endured on his journey. Actually, Homer was not written by Homer but by another man of that name.

Adultery is one of the Ten Commandments. It is a bad thing. Adultery is when you tell people you're older than you really are.

God created the world in six days. On the seventh day, he was arrested.

Motherhood Is Not For Sissies

Every May, as Mother's Day approaches, my thoughts turn to how a woman's life changes the moment she learns that she is to become a mother. Motherhood is a joy, but it is a tough job. If it wasn't hard work, it wouldn't start out with a process called "labor."

Pregnancy is a beautiful thing, but for me, it was the end of any feelings of control I'd ever had over my own body. From the very beginning, my child took over…completely. I felt like I had a tag team of midget wrestlers rolling around in my midsection. I joined a "new mommies-to-be" exercise class. We met twice a week to do our expectant mother exercises. For forty-five minutes, the other mommies bent and stretched to the music. My workout was trying to lift myself out of the chair. While the others touched their toes, I attempted to find mine. Our workouts took about the same amount of time, and produced the same amount of sweat.

When my daughter was born, she was a beautiful, perfect little angel. So of course, I decided that she needed a sibling, and soon afterwards, her sister arrived. Mothers do that…we have more than one child before we realize that these cherubic babes soon turn into teenagers!

It doesn't take long for a mother to realize who is in charge…it's the children, of course! Your whole identity is wrapped up in your offspring. When I had been a mommy for six years, I began to realize that more often than not, my conversations included quotes from Dr. Seuss. I spoke in rhyme, carried animal crackers and wind-up alligators in my purse, and constantly wiped dirty little hands and noses…even if they didn't belong to my children. I'll never forget the look on the face of the man standing behind me in the grocery checkout line, when I held a hanky to his nose and told him to stop sniffing and blow.

I couldn't remember wearing a dress without a sticky fingerprint on it, or going to a movie that didn't feature talking animals or enchanted forests. I could vaguely recall attending college classes and reading books that didn't have pictures. I was pretty sure that I had once been able to speak about world affairs, but at this point, I had come down with Mother Goose Syndrome.

As the children grew, I became aware of the powerful leverage tool, which is passed down from generation to generation of parents. It is the gift of guilt…the gift that keeps on giving. It is a way for us to regain some of the control that was lost when we brought another little personality into the world. The talent of guilt giving is something you receive immediately upon becoming a parent. It doesn't start out to be a negative thing; as a matter of fact, when a mother sees her baby for the first time, she wants nothing more than to protect it and keep it from harm. Guilt giving can be an effective tool in this endeavor, and it works beautifully when combined with the proper doses of threats and bribery. These are all components of a larger concept called "Motherism." If mothers did not utilize these techniques every now and then, we would have no defense against the sharp and crafty minds of our children. They are younger, quicker, and have more energy. We can't always keep up with them so we have to use any means available to get them to listen. Face it, when a five year old is getting ready to shave the dog, sometimes the only thing that will stop him in his tracks is being reminded that Santa Claus doesn't visit children who give their pets mohawks. Parents have to live by their wits!

I always believed my mother when she told me what was going to happen if I didn't listen to her. For years, I wouldn't make a face or cross my eyes for over ten seconds, knowing full well that if I did, that expression would be frozen on me forever. When I was sixteen and first driving, I was pulled over by a policeman for speeding. When I saw the flashing lights behind me, my heart raced and I frantically contemplated making a break for it. It wasn't the speeding ticket that caused my terror, it was the bags of Twinkies, Ding Dongs, and Yoo Hoos that I had hidden in my glove compartment. My mother had told me that possession of junk food was illegal in our state. I feared that my stash of contraband would be discovered and I'd be swinging a hammer on a chain gang!

Guilt and other "motherisms" stay with you for a long time. I was twenty-eight years old before I'd even step in a puddle until an hour after I had eaten, and it took an overnight camp out to prove to me that your teeth won't really fall out if you miss one night of flossing.

When you're a kid, you never think you're going to grow up to be a travel agent for guilt trips, but it seems that the minute they place that new baby in your arms, a force greater than yourself takes over and you automatically become fluent in "Motherese." We use this power to convey important points to our children. I couldn't believe my own ears when I heard myself tell my youngest child that her thumb would fall off if she continued to suck it. Motherese just becomes a part of you; you can't control it and you can't stop it. In one afternoon, I caught myself telling my daughters that if they played with the straws from their drinks, they were going to put someone's eye out, that their hands would blow off if they stuck them out of the car window, and that swallowing gum would permanently stick their insides together.

When I bribed my eldest to eat vegetables by telling her that she would grow breasts quicker if she ate asparagus, I knew I needed help. I decided to try a support group that my friend had mentioned to me. It was called Mom-Anon, and it was for people like me, who spoke in Motherese clichés and had fallen to the ways of guilt giving, threats, and bribes.

When I called for information about their meetings, the receptionist answered, "Good afternoon, thanks for calling Mom-Anon, and it wouldn't hurt you to call your own mother every now and then. May we help you?"

"When is the next meeting?" I asked.

She answered, "Tomorrow, at four o'clock sharp. Don't be late and wear a sweater!"

The next day, I entered the meeting hall and was greeted by a lovely lady who introduced herself and said, "Welcome to Mom-Anon, you look tired, have you been eating right?" Then she put her hand on my forehead to check for fever.

There were women of all ages and types there, all with one thing in common...we were mothers. The meeting began with refreshments, and as I sat nibbling on little sandwiches, I was reminded twice to chew each bite at least twenty times, and thrice, I was admonished for leaving a crust of bread on my plate, when there were starving children in Bangladesh.

The keynote speaker talked about the need to rid ourselves of the guilt that plagued us, and that we were passing on to our own children. What she said made a lot of sense, until she closed by stating that none of us would be having these problems now, if we had only listened to our mothers.

Things became clear to me, at that point. "Motherisms," like guilt, threats, and bribes are a part of the genetic code of mothers. It is triggered by labor contractions. It is a continuum that spins from generation to generation, and when you really think about it, it's kind of comfortable to know that some things never change.

Now that my own children are grown and I am a grandmother, I have been on both the receiving and giving ends of "Motherisms." I speak and understand "Motherese." Now I am waiting for the day when I will hear one of my daughters tell her children that living in a messy bedroom gives you acne. I would also like to publicly apologize to my mother for the time that I let the dog wear her new cashmere sweater.

And to my beautiful daughters, I leave these words…"Now it's your turn."

Conflict: Refuse and Defuse It!

People aren't necessarily born "funny". A baby may LOOK funny…I have seen pictures of myself as a newborn and believe me, I was pretty funny. I looked like a cross between Yoda, of Star Wars fame, and Winston Churchill. But appearances aside, people usually have to develop humor skills. There is a difference between being funny and communicating a sense of humor.

Oddly enough, humor often springs from unpleasantness. Many successful comedians had difficult childhoods and learned to use humor to overcome their hardships. Humor and difficulty are actually closely related. Sometimes when we face conflict, we find that the situation actually lends itself to humor because that may be the only way we can maintain our perspective and gain strength to go forward. It is no mistake that some of the funniest movies ever made and comedy routines ever performed came about during the years following the Great Depression, and we all know that Bob Hope and his U.S.O. shows were an important morale booster for our troops overseas. Laughter gives us a respite from the pain and allows us to regroup and get back on our feet again.

We must nurture our sense of humor and keep it well conditioned. It is a valuable tool to keep on hand, and like any tool, must be maintained and honed.

Fortunately, many corporations are realizing the value of a healthy sense of humor in their employees. One corporate executive told me that while interviewing a perspective employee, he makes a mental note of how long it takes for the interviewee to somehow communicate a sense of humor. He acknowledges a sense of humor as an asset in any business setting because it defuses negativity and is instrumental in conflict resolution.

As parents, we have a wonderful opportunity to teach our kids to tap into their inner resources of humor. One year, I was teaching Junior High students and there were two young men who just could not get along with each other. Their mutual antagonism was disruptive, frustrating, and sometimes downright frightening. It didn't take long for me to lose patience with the situation and besides, both were physically larger than I, making it difficult to separate them when they actually came to blows. One day, out of sheer frustration, I offered them a challenge. I told them that the next time their tempers flared, they were to stand face to face and before any nasty words or punches were thrown, each was to say one thing that he liked about the other. Of course, they looked at me in disbelief, and the other students snickered, rolled their eyes heavenward, and made typical Junior High noises. Since I had dared them, the two boys accepted the challenge. The next day, as usual, a conflict arose between the two and it didn't take long for the class to remind them of their challenge. I will never forget the amazing scene that followed. With red faces, clenched fists, and wild eyes, these two stood nose to nose, desperately trying to think of one single thing to say in order to make good their dare and commence with the fighting. Finally, in exasperation, one of them blurted out the only positive attribute that he could conjure up about his foe... "You're the only one I know who can burp louder than I can." It didn't take long for everyone to burst into laughter, including the two challengers. As a matter of fact, we all laughed so long and hard, that the point of the conflict was forgotten and the negativity dissipated.

The class agreed to adopt the "Smile When You Say That" challenge, and it cast a whole new light on arguments and confrontations in our classroom. The best part of this incident was the long-term results. Throughout the year, I observed students employing this technique when confrontations arose on the playground or other areas outside of the classroom. I have since used the same concept in dealing with negative people in my personal life and in touchy business situations. If I force myself to think of one positive attribute about the person who has angered or hurt me, it allows me some time to rethink my negative feelings and evaluate the situation. I usually find that it doesn't merit wasting energy or harboring toxic emotions.

The trick to using humor in conflict resolution is to shift attention away from the problem, and refocus. A person cannot entertain anger and amusement at the same time, so, if the angry person is made to chuckle, the hostility is lessened and the direction of the situation can be altered. If an argument is escalating in one direction, humor stops it and turns it around. Humor changes expectations and reduces, resolves, and prevents conflict.

As a parent, your imagination is the key to unlocking ways to solve problems and settle disputes. One innovative mother of five, teaches her children to juggle with cheesecloth scarves. When an altercation occurs, she tells the involved parties that they may continue their argument only after spending five minutes juggling scarves. This exercise shifts their attention, because one cannot successfully juggle if one's mind is elsewhere. Just breaking the negative tension goes a long way toward defusing the situation, and, the children usually find themselves giggling as they stand there, throwing scarves into the air.

Another effective exercise which allows kids to step back and reevaluate anger is the "Mad List." When someone becomes overcome with anger and frustration, a healthy way to vent some steam is to have him write all the things about which he is angry. Instruct him that he is to write as fast and furiously as possible...non-stop for five minutes. Set a timer or let him know when the time is up and by then, most of the angry energy should be expended.

There are always options and alternatives. If children learn early on that there are other ways to deal with disappointment and anger, their chances for handling problems in later life are improved. Besides, it makes your life as a parent easier!

"Few would deny that the capacity for humor, like hope, is one of humanity's most potent antidotes for the woes of Pandora's box."– George Valliant

---

Having Dating-Age Daughters Can Be Hazardous To A Father's Health

June always makes me think of two things...Father's Day and weddings. In my mind, these two thoughts are a natural fit because I have two daughters who recently were brides and I have a husband who is the father of the two brides and he didn't want to give them away. At both weddings, I believe he had an escape route all mapped out and was ready to smuggle the bride out through a tunnel he had dug with a spoon! For some reason, each of the girls elected to stay in the church and go through with the ceremony.

Fathers and daughters are a fascinating duo. Nothing reduces a man into mush quite like holding his newborn baby girl, admiring her delicate little features and feeling her tiny fingers wrap around his thumb. Nothing, that is, except watching her leave the house for a first date.

Nothing could have prepared us for our daughters' dating years. To begin with, it was terribly confusing. Someone should issue a dating dictionary to parents to assist them in defining the current dating terms. There were friends who were boys, and boys who were friends, then there were the boyfriends, who were clearly in another category entirely. Someone needs to come out with a crash course in "teen relationships." It seemed that "going out" was different from "going with," which was certainly not to be confused with "seeing someone," which was not to be mistaken for "dating." It made me wonder about the possible danger of confusion if the relationship ever progressed to marriage. Would "married to" be the same as "wedded with?" Would "I do" really mean you do…or would it merely imply that you might?

When you are the parent of teenage girls who insist upon associating with boys, you must be prepared to see many unpleasant things. You must accept the fact that although you gave birth to the most perfect child on the planet, and spent sums equaling the national debt just to keep her that way, she will choose to date the most far out creatures she can possibly find. She will search high and low to seek out the hairiest, gum-snappiest, most ill mannered specimen available. And if he speaks only in monosyllabic words and grunts…so much the better.

It is a pretty dependable rule of thumb, that the more you express displeasure at the sight of the hairball camped in your living room with his feet on the couch, the tighter your daughter will cling to it.

One evening, my husband happened to look out the window just in time to see something creeping up our front walk. "Good golly!" he hollered, "Those roaches are getting bigger and bolder every year! This one is ringing the doorbell. Quick, get the bug spray!"

Our oldest daughter bounded down the hall, shoved her father aside and flung open the door. "Mom and Dad," she began, "this is Slug." My husband tried to slam the door on him. I grabbed his arm. "We can't let that in our house," he whispered, "those things travel in packs. Once you open the door to one, they all start coming out of the woodwork."

"We have to respect her choice in friends," I said, "but hurry and get some plastic to put on the couch before he sits down."

My daughter clung tightly to the creature, although I wasn't sure if it was voluntary or if she was stuck in some of his matted hair. I was, however, determined to show her that I had trust in her judgment. I tried to tell myself that this mass of dirty fur on my couch was some mother's child. Of course, so was Rosemary's Baby.

"Well, Slug," I began, "do you go to our daughter's school?"

"Nope," growled Slug.

"Have you lived here in town for long?" I tried.

"Nope."

"Have you any brothers or sisters?"

"Nope."

Adjust Your Attitude

"Have you ever seen a bathtub?" my husband interjected.

"Daddy!" scolded our daughter.

My husband could not be stopped. "Can I get you anything, Slug?" Coffee, tea, soft drink, tick dip?" With that, our firstborn jumped to her feet, glared at us and lovingly led the Slug out of the door and into the night.

"Well, now you've done it!" I hissed, "you've permanently cemented the bond between them. Don't you know that even if she didn't like him before, you've put your mark of disapproval on him and now she has no choice but to plan a future with him? It's the teenage girl's credo…'Annoy Thy Parents.' She has to follow through with it."

"I don't get it," he whimpered.

Don't you remember, when you first came to my house, my father tried to hit you with a broom?"

"Yes, I recall that."

"And when you came over for dinner, he put earplugs in his ears and refused to even talk to you."

"Yeah, I remember. He wouldn't pass me any food and kept putting his chicken bones on my plate."

"Well," I said, "I never really liked you much until then…but as soon as my father started to treat you badly, you became more attractive to me."

"That's why you agreed to marry me that day he accidentally ran over my foot with the lawn mower?" he asked.

"Right!" I said.

From that point on, my husband could not do enough for Slug. He became obsessed; believing that the more he welcomed Slug, the farther away our daughter would push the beast. It was really quite heartwarming, watching him grit his teeth while welcoming Slug into our home, carrying on one-sided conversations with him, dusting the chairs with flea powder when he left; all for the sake of our daughter.

Slug became a permanent fixture in our home, and a large fixture at that. He was a big boy…approximately the size of a small county. His feet were huge; people have sailed the Atlantic in smaller crafts. He was on our couch so often, I began to believe I was going to have to have him upholstered. I knew that my husband was close to his breaking point. He now had a glazed look in his eyes and a few tics that hadn't been there before, but he hung in there, for the good of his little girl.

One night, about three months after the Slug invasion, our child came into our bedroom.

"I've got to talk to you guys," she said sternly. "I can't go on like this. I am sick to death of Slug; he's running our house. I never would have even gone out with him after the first time, except that Daddy seemed to like him so much."

"What?" my husband choked on the cheese doodle he was munching. His face was contorted and his ears were red.

"I really tried, for your sake, Daddy," continued our daughter. "But you'll just have to get over him because I'm throwing him out. And I'm really surprised at you two. I thought you would want better for me than a guy like Slug."

I didn't even have to look at him. I could feel the angry heat radiating from my husband's side of the bed. I closed my eyes and pretended to sleep.

"You and your psychology," he snarled, "She never even liked him! I have just spent three months of my life endangering my physical and mental health, courting something that looks like it crawled out of a vacuum cleaner bag. The couch is no longer usable by humanoids, and I have wasted a quarter of a year being nice to something that my daughter didn't even want in the first place."

"Well," I sniffed, "You should be happy that our daughter has more discriminating tastes than we thought she did. Besides, it was good practice; we still have another daughter entering the dating zone, you know."

A few months later, my husband answered the door to something that looked like a refugee from an irrigation ditch.

"Mom and Dad," began our youngest daughter, "This is Worm."

My husband never said a word, but I will never forget the sight of him chasing Worm down the street with a fly swatter. Today, my husband and I give the following advice to parents of dating daughters: When your little girl brings home something that could be either her date or the school mascot; when her new boyfriend's career ambition is to be a speed bump; or when her "significant other" does not own a shirt with sleeves and believes that a job would dry up his creative juices and cloud his destiny…exercise self control for five minutes. Then, whip out the bug zapper and let him have it!

Fortunately, the Slugs and Worms slithered out of the lives of our daughters and we watched them choose wonderful young men as their life's mates. We are fortunate to have two sons-in-law who speak in complete sentences, hold down jobs, and use utensils when they eat. Even my husband likes them.

As Father's Day approaches, however, I can't help but remember those early years. Like I said, nothing reduces a man into mush quite like holding his newborn baby girl, or watching her leave the house on a first date…unless it's walking her down the aisle and giving her away to another man.

Full "Esteem" Ahead

Very few people would argue with the fact that healthy self-esteem makes a major difference in the quality of a person's life. Children with low self-esteem are likely to take this handicap with them into their adult lives. When self-esteem is low, the ability to find success in relationships and life skills is greatly reduced. People don't just happen to have a healthy self-concept, the seed of self-esteem must be planted and nurtured until it takes root and begins to grow.

Studies have shown that high self-esteem is not necessarily related to family, wealth, social class, ethnicity, or education. It comes from the quality of relationships that exist between children and the people who play a significant part in their lives. It is recognition of respect and worthiness, which gives children the ability to focus on themselves as a valuable part of the community and the world. When a child knows that he is seen as an asset to the group, his self-image reflects this knowledge.

As parents, we are aware that building a child's self-esteem should be incorporated into the daily routine. It is a cumulative process, which is a part of every day and every activity. Our goal is to implant our children with confidence that is rooted so deeply, it will never fall out! In order for a child to experience a positive feeling in the world, the home environment must support that attitude.

Trying to effectively raise a child without humor is about as successful as nailing Jell-O to a wall. Studies show that laughter is an effective parenting tool. It gets both parent and child through some potentially nerve-racking situations. I'm sure we've all been there…you can either laugh or cry.

Parents are often afraid that using humor will distract and disrupt, or possibly undermine their authority. Actually, the opposite is true. Well-placed humor will enhance the family experience and add to the parents' effectiveness. When children are enjoying themselves and feeling comfortable, they are more likely to cooperate, and they learn to take themselves lightly while taking their responsibilities seriously.

Smiling is contagious and it's the best fuel ever discovered to fire up that "esteem engine!" We might even say that it is the necessary tool to build up a "full head of esteem!"

Adjust Your Attitude

Lesson Five:
Laughter and Perspective

Humor provides perspective…it allows you to stand back and look at the big picture.

You know you'll look back on a tense situation and laugh; so why wait? LAUGH NOW!

This letter from a college student demonstrates the power of using humor to help us step back and see our problems in a different light:

Dear Mom and Dad,

I'm sorry that I have not written, but all my stationery was destroyed when the dorm burned down. I am now out of the hospital and the doctor said that I will soon be fully recovered. I also have moved in with the boy who rescued me, since most of my things were destroyed in the fire.

Oh yes. I know that you always wanted a grandchild, so you will be pleased to know that I am pregnant and you will have one soon.

Love,
Jodie

Then, the postscript:

P.S. There was no fire, my health is fine and I am not pregnant. In fact, I do not even have a boyfriend. However, I did get a D in French and a C in Math and Chemistry and I just wanted to make sure that you keep it all in perspective.

"Life is a tragedy when seen in close up, but a comedy in a long shot." – Charlie Chaplin

---

Our Perceptions Control What We Do

54

OPPORTUNITYISNOWHERE

The above is a "run-on" sentence. There are two ways to read it—depending on your perspective. On the line below, separate the words.

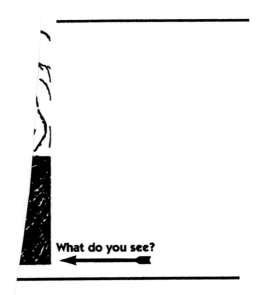

What do you see?

ord 'Crisis' is composed of two characters
ther represents opportunity."– John Kennedy

...o matter how bad things are; find cheer in the ...he next time you're slammed with a depression ...ou'll be surprised at how lightening up your ...uth. For example:

...feeling unattractive and wishing that we could ...in at yourself…"I can't stand even looking in the ...**ould be worse**…I could have been twins!"

...ws and There's Good News

...) put things into proper perspective. There are ... and you may as well focus on the positive! Sit ... situation in a creative and humorous way. For

...ngs a leak and you have a kitchen full of water. You ...**he bad news** is that my kitchen is full of water, **the** ...door swimming pool I've always wanted!

Things that Really Irritate Me

Sometimes it is healthy to vent your frustrations by putting them down on paper and acknowledging how much they bug you. I will start you out with a few of my own, and you may add to the list.

1. How they put skinny women wearing string bikinis on the cover of sports magazines...like it's really a sport to wear dental floss! What's wrong with turtle necked, long sleeved support bathing suits with feet, anyway?

2. When I break a tooth eating yogurt. Yogurt!

3. Control top panty hose that exercise absolutely no control.

4. _____

5. _____

6. _____

7. _____

8. _____

9. _____

10. _____

Lesson Six: Laughter in Adversity

We cannot always control the environment, but we **can** control the variables within our environment, such as how we have fun, how we relate to difficult people, how long we allow ourselves to feel angry, depressed, or otherwise miserable, and how we laugh at ourselves. It has been said that things work out best for those who make the best of the way things work out. It's hard to argue with that one.

Everyone seems to be searching for happiness. What is happiness, anyway? It usually is a reaction to a situation that seems to make us feel good for a while. Happiness is fleeting. What we ought to be looking for is a sense of peace. Peace is that feeling deep within that makes us comfortable and able to access the joy that comes our way. I think the laughing spirit comes from having a sense of peace. If we have it, we don't always have to be waiting and wondering when the next ecstatic moment will arrive. We can just sit back and enjoy what life has to offer.

---

*"Every good thought you think is contributing its share
to the ultimate result of your life."– Grenville Klieser*

"The mind in its own place and in itself can make heaven of hell or hell of heaven."– Milton

---

*"If you wish to glimpse inside a human soul and get to know a man...
just watch him laugh. If he laughs well, he's a good man."– Dostoevski*

---

*"Watch your thoughts; they become words. Watch your words; they become actions.
Watch your actions, they become habits. Watch your habits; they become character.
Watch your character; it becomes your destiny."– Frank Outlaw*

All Hail The Mighty "Worry Warrior"

I am an accomplished worrier. Like anyone who is an expert in their field, I carefully polish and hone my worry skills. I am not content to be a mediocre worrier therefore I am constantly perfecting and fine tuning my technique. You might say that I am in training to be a world class worrier. Those less talented in the sport of worrying may not realize that it is not merely a mindless activity consisting of a few well-placed sighs and brow furrows. No, indeed! Worrying is an all-encompassing exercise involving every body part and emotion. When done regularly and properly, it causes the heart to pound, the sweat glands to pump, the stomach to knot, the face to contort, and the mind to become dysfunctional, shutting out any possibility of hope and focusing totally on the object of concern.

The sport of worrying has no season; therefore it is possible to participate at any time of the year, preferably all times of the year. The true marathon worrier, if properly trained, is able to deflect all attempts of well meaning friends, and discount all logical and comforting explanations of the futility of worry. A true Worry Warrior will carry on despite efforts of others to defuse the problem.

It is particularly gratifying to worry about those things over which we have absolutely no control. This takes intense concentration and endurance, and the physical benefits are just icing on the cake! The well earned badges which label a Worry Warrior are reward enough; the stooped shoulders, lined face, wrinkled brow, and pained expression are worth every minute of training, but imagine the feeling of exultation one experiences if he or she is blessed with a little nervous tic!

I am not the only Worry Warrior I know. I have two friends, who are a couple, and are contenders for the title of American Worry Gladiator. They are in their forties and she worries about having enough body in her hair. He worries about having enough hair on his body. They both worry about becoming middle aged. I keep telling them that to worry about that is to assume that they are going to live to be in their eighties, therefore justifying that they are now at the midpoint. In actuality they may not live that long at all, in which case, they would have really hit middle age years ago and sailed through it with flying colors. I have now alleviated one of their concerns. As a friend, it is my duty.

Worrying is recyclable which makes it something you can always count on. And it, like guilt, is the gift that keeps on giving. Families can pass it on from generation to generation, provided that it is cherished and protected like the family jewels. Parents worry about their children; children worry about being embarrassed by their parents. When those children become parents, they worry about **their** children who worry about being embarrassed by **their** parents who used to be the children. See how it works?

We Worry Warriors are a selective group. We must be willing to constantly wade and wallow in the wastewater of worldly woe and never be tempted to grab onto that life preserver of hope, lest we be rescued and never again have an excuse to make ourselves miserable.

I know that if I weave for myself a web of worry, I will never be disappointed when things turn out for the worst. I can always hold high the hope of becoming the patron saint of worry. I can just envision the likeness of me, dressed in shades of black, bent under the weight of my own sorrow; painted on black velvet and hanging in the homes of lesser Worry Warriors worldwide. Sometimes, though, I worry that I won't look my best on velvet.

Slightly Irregular

The other day I was shopping and came upon a display of underwear just piled up on a table under a sign that read SLIGHTLY IRREGULAR. Intrigued by the possibilities of irregular underwear, I shuffled through the pile, wondering if I would find bras with three cups or panties with sleeves. I was surprised to find seemingly normal underwear, with no distinguishing characteristics.

I asked the sales person to explain to me the meaning of the description and she said that this was underwear that had hidden flaws, but no one was really sure just what they were. All she knew was that the factory had labeled them slightly irregular, so the store marked them at half price and set them out on a table. I inquired as to whether one had to be slightly irregular to fit into them, and she said she didn't think so. So I purchased five pair of slightly irregulars, wondering if the irregularity was that they would fall apart after being worn for three hours or perhaps self-destruct in the clothes dryer.

You'll be glad to know that I have worn my new underwear, and everything is just fine. Now, maybe that is because they are only SLIGHTLY irregular as opposed to totally irregular; I can't say. All I know is that I got twice as many pair of slightly irregulars as I would have been able to purchase had they been regular and full price.

The point of this is that we sometimes plan for ourselves, a life that is perfect. There is certainly nothing wrong with this, we should envision perfection. But the truth of the matter is that perfection very rarely happens. The fact is…our lives are usually slightly irregular, and when they are, we sometimes discount the worth of the imperfections.

Am I extracting a life lesson from my underwear? Well, yes, in a way, I am. When things don't go as planned, how often we throw up our hands and proclaim our failures as worthless! We discount our not so perfect experiences, our slightly irregulars, and think of them as inferior.

What I have learned over the years, is that sometimes, in hindsight, it is difficult to distinguish between the good days and the bad days. I guess it's because even though I hate to admit it, I have gotten more out of my bad days. My not so perfect, "slightly irregular" experiences have been the ones that have caused me to reevaluate my goals, put things into proper perspective and reaffirm that I will live through my failures and disappointments.

We need to learn that one of the best things we can do for ourselves is to set goals and strive for success, but one of the most harmful things we can do is to feel a sense of failure if we fall short of those goals. In striving for perfection, we learn to accept and even embrace our imperfections.

So ends my "life is like slightly irregular underwear" story. I hope it makes sense to you. I leave this topic with one final thought…while it's always nice to have lingerie from Victoria's Secret; we can also benefit from "slightly irregulars." And besides, who knows…Victoria's secret just may be that she is "slightly irregular!"

YOU ARE INVITED TO A PITY PARTY

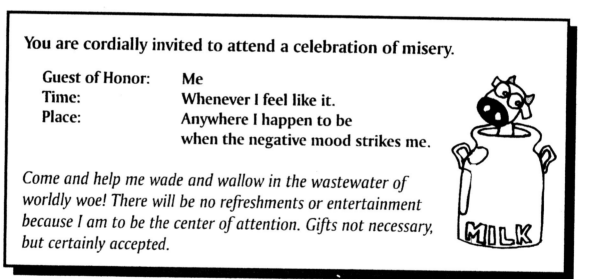

You are cordially invited to attend a celebration of misery.

Guest of Honor: Me
Time: **Whenever I feel like it.**
Place: **Anywhere I happen to be**
when the negative mood strikes me.

Come and help me wade and wallow in the wastewater of worldly woe! There will be no refreshments or entertainment because I am to be the center of attention. Gifts not necessary, but certainly accepted.

Would you ever expect to receive something like this in the mail? Probably not, yet people extend such invitations all the time!

Let's face it; we all love to moan and groan now and then, and it makes it much more gratifying to have an audience. The truth is, I don't know a single soul who doesn't occasionally enjoy being the center of attention and the object of everyone's sympathy.

We may not want to admit it, but when we're feeling lousy, we kind of like to take everyone down with us, right? Be honest now, when we're wading and wallowing,

Adjust Your Attitude

the last thing we want to hear is someone cooing about how things really aren't that bad! Most of us feel like we deserve to be down in the dumps and no one is going to cheat us out of it! That's just human nature and I'd be willing to bet that even Mary Poppins slipped into the pits once in a blue moon.

We just need to be careful that allowing ourselves to give into negativity doesn't become a life long pattern. We can count on our friends to be there for support when we really need them, but even the most long-suffering friends will turn down invitations to our pity parties if we issue them too often. It doesn't take many tearful laments of "Woe is me, nobody cares!" before we realize that nobody does (Just kidding!) Other people can only help us if we choose to help ourselves.

A while ago, I learned an incredibly valuable life lesson from a very dear friend who was losing her battle with cancer. While visiting her in her hospital room, I was voicing my anger at that ugly disease which was ravaging her body. In the midst of my ranting, she spoke up and said something I will never forget. She told me that I needed to wake up and straighten out my priorities. She said that she and the other terminally ill patients were not dying…they were living, because they had come to terms with their conditions and were determined to live the remainder of their days to the fullest extent possible. And then she looked at me in the eye and said, "You, my friend are so engulfed in anger and fear. You are the one who has forgotten how to live."

Until that moment, I had never seen things in that light, but I now know truer words were never spoken. Most of us admit to being a little afraid of dying, but in actuality, I think that many are afraid of living!

We become so set in our ways that we forget to take risks. I don't mean bungee jumping or running naked in the streets. Personally, I might try bungee jumping, but I value my fellow humans too much to subject them to my unclothed body. The risks to which I am referring are the ones which put us (or so we think) in danger of appearing silly or unprofessional. The fear of this often prohibits us from allowing our inner child to pop out. We are afraid to risk knocking down the walls we build around ourselves which keep people from getting too close, because to do so would make us vulnerable to failure and rejection.

So, we keep our true, child-like spirits trapped inside and then bemoan the fact that adulthood is no fun and we miss our childhood. We regularly send invitations to our Pity Parties and then wonder why no one comes or sends gifts.

"The laughing person is open to the world; the crying person only sees his own suffering."– Helmuth Plessner

MEDITATIONS AND MANTRAS OF MISERY

☹ I have low self-esteem because I deserve it.

☹ Today is the first day of the rest of my lousy life…of course, it could be the last day because tragedy is never far away.

☹ If I seek and find my inner child of the past, she will probably not want to hang around with me.

☹ When I count my blessings, I realize how few I really have.

☹ Beauty is in the eye of the beholder, unless the beholder happens to be looking at me.

☹ Life cannot get me down if I am already down and plan to stay there.

☹ I realize that if I am unhappy with who I am, I have the power to change, but it probably won't make any difference because I will still be a loser.

☹ I know that I should be my own best friend, but I am not really that crazy about me.

☹ The best things in life are free, but so are the worst.

☹ I try to live up to my potential until I realize that I have no potential.

☹ I know that I will never lose control of my life because I never had control in the first place.

☹ Some things in life were never meant to be and my happiness is one of them.

☹ I am determined to always expect the worst so I will never be disappointed…even though I deserve to be disappointed because I am unworthy.

Tame Those Trolls

Do you remember the story of The Three Billy Goats Gruff? There was a family of goats who wanted to cross over a bridge, but a nasty troll lived under the bridge and threatened to eat them.

I believe that we all have trolls living under our bridges. We need to cross these bridges to get to where we're going and we want to cross, but we're frightened by the trolls, so we turn back and don't ever reach our goals.

I, personally, have many trolls. They take the form of fear, insecurity, worry, guilt, envy, and many more of their relatives. The trolls sit by my bridges and threaten to eat me if I try to pass, so I often back up and give up on my hopes and dreams.

There is a major troll; quite possibly the Troll King, who lives under almost everyone's bridge. His name is Negativity, and he is very powerful. One reason he is so powerful, is that he can change his shape and size, and is very sneaky. He encourages the other trolls to perpetuate the myths that many of us already believe; for instance, to ask for what you want is selfish and to show anger is to be sinful, childish, and unprofessional.

Trolls tend to appear and do their best work when we are very close to taking steps in a positive direction. This is when they show their true colors and encourage us to surround ourselves with self-limiting thoughts. Sometimes they convince us that we are not worthy of success and happiness, but should embrace anxiety, worry, and guilt.

How do we tame our trolls and drive them back under the bridges where they belong? One way is simply to be aware; to pay attention to how you are. That is different than analyzing yourself to pieces and trying to figure out why you are the way you are. It is more productive to spend time being in contact with your current experiences and simply taking note of them, than to worry about why you're feeling a certain way. The first step in troll taming is to be aware and be creative. Awareness is a valuable tool, because at any point in time, we can choose to focus our awareness away from our problems and toward our positive ideas, dreams, and happy memories.

Trolls like to frighten us, so it really throws a wrench in their plans when we simply recognize them and then move away from them. Trolls often try to hide behind physical and emotional symptoms such as headaches, ulcers, neuroses, and other ailments. Once you begin to feel any tension in your body, you have a clue that your troll is present. Notice the effect it is having on you and begin relaxation exercises or do something that makes you happy. Acknowledge the troll, then move away from it.

Trolls want us to "should" all over ourselves! "Should" just might be one of the most damaging words we can have in our vocabulary, because it sets us up for failure. All the energy we expend in thinking about what we should have done or the way we should behave or the things we should have accomplished, is energy that could better be spent in creative thought.

Without a doubt, however, the very best and most effective anti-troll device available to us is our sense of humor. When we are able to access joy in adversity and put things into proper perspective, it's like using RAID for trolls...laughter kills 'em dead!

Infamous Trolls to Watch Out For

☹ I must be perfect and have every-one's approval.

☹ I really don't deserve to have good fortune, especially if someone I love is less fortunate.

☹ If everything is going too well, I'd better beware, for trouble is near!

☹ If I try anything new or take any risks, I will probably fail.

☹ Other people have more abilities than I and it would be better to keep in the background, since I have nothing to contribute.

☹ My happiness is dependent upon on other people.

☹ The guilt that I carry around is atonement for my mistakes.

☹ I should be content with what I have and not ever hope for anything more, because to ask or expect any more out of life would be selfish.

☹ I must be constantly on guard against appearing foolish.

Lesson Seven: Laughter and Negativity

Humor breaks negative patterns and defuses potentially explosive situations. Living with negativity is stifling, suffocating, and restrictive. It is like trying to climb up a mountain while wearing cement shoes. You'll end up going nowhere fast!

Well-placed, appropriate humor can reframe a problem and make it manageable. It can bridge the gap between people and create an environment which is conducive to success, compatibility, and positive results.

Most of our negativity comes from scripts we write for ourselves, based on past experiences and fear of failure. Just because we didn't get the results for which we were hoping the last time we tried something, doesn't mean the same thing will happen again. Our past does not equal our future. If something isn't working, try another approach.

So often, we are like the man who packs his own lunch every day and then complains about what he has in his lunch pail. We don't give ourselves credit for being able to break a negative pattern. It's just easier to blame other people or circumstances.

We can learn to short circuit the blues using positive affirmations. Accepting our right to happiness is probably the biggest hurdle for most of us. If we refuse to make negativity an option; if we choose to be in a positive mood; if we remind ourselves that we can deal with anything if we keep a sense of humor; we can come closer to claiming our well-deserved peace of mind.

"The person who has a sense of humor is not just more relaxed in the face of potentially stressful situations, but is more flexible in his approach."– John Morreall in "Taking Laughter Seriously"

"You have no idea of the poor opinion I have of myself and how little I deserve it."– W.S. Gilbert

---

"We are, perhaps, uniquely among the earth's creatures, the worrying animal. We worry away our lives, fearing the future, discontent with the present, unable to take in the idea of dying, unable to sit still."– Lewis Thomas

---

Dealing With Negative People?
"Humor" Them!

We all are occasionally forced to deal with negative people. You know the ones…the Certified Chronic Complainers. These delightful souls are experts at taking any given situation and adding just the right touch of negativity. A pinch of pessimism here, a dash of despair there; just enough to cloud any hope of a successful condition.

These "Triple Cs," as we shall call them, come in all shapes, sizes, ages, genders, and levels of danger. They are the ones who will always have an answer for your well-intentioned comments. For instance, in response to your statement, "The best things in life are free," they will counter with "Yeah, well the worst things in life are free, too!"

Sometimes, their negativity seems harmless enough; even funny at times. But left unchecked, particularly in a workplace or family situation, it can grow like a malignancy and cause tremendous damage. Consider the staff of an elementary school, which called me in for an Attitude Adjustment seminar. As the attendees were entering the lecture hall, one of the students' parents approached me with these words: "I certainly hope this session works, because the people at this school really hate each other!"

I was dumbfounded and asked him to elaborate. He told me that the staff had once been cohesive, but one particular person had come on board who had poisoned the positive atmosphere and pitted co-workers against each other. He painted a bleak picture of the future of the school, saying the poison had spread into the community. The students were aware of the friction between their teachers and the parents were concerned by the hostility to which their children were being exposed.

It is absolutely amazing what one little seed of negativity can do. Imagine that you are looking at an expansive white canvas, and suddenly, a tiny little black dot appears in the middle. Immediately, your eyes are drawn to that little speck, which now mars the otherwise spotless background. So it is, when even one negative person infiltrates a staff or an office, or any other situation. If we are not prepared to move away from it, negativity sucks us in and makes us a part of its vortex.

Possibly, the most difficult situation to resolve is dealing with a negative person…when that person happens to be you! Sometimes we get ourselves stuck in a little spiral of negativity, and might not even be aware of how often we make little snide comments about a co-worker, or complain about our situation.

It is important to remember that negativity stems from fear. Anyone who is caught in its web is a victim. Fear is a darkroom in which negativity is developed. By refusing to be affected and brought down by the anti-positive forces, and by attempting to understand what is causing the anger, misery, and complaining, we are taking important steps toward "negating the negative."

"The strangest and most fantastic thing about negative emotions is that people actually worship them."– P.D. Ouspensky

---

Negate The Negative

I think that perhaps lyricist Johnny Mercer said it best: "You gotta accentuate the positive, eliminate the negative, latch onto the affirmative; don't mess with Mr. In-between."

Most of us don't want to admit it, but we are addicted to negative thinking. There are many reasons why this is so, but perhaps they are not so important as the effort to simply kick the habit.

A while back, someone pointed out to me, that when I am spending my time in worry, anger, frustration, fear, or any other negative mode, I am renting out space in my brain to unhealthy thoughts. That means that every little brain cell being occupied by a negative thought is unavailable to accommodate a positive one. Since I, personally, am not sure just how many brain cells I own, the idea of running a boarding house for dark and evil little thoughts is not appealing to me. I don't wish for my brain to be a slum.

I don't believe that most of us really realize just how much energy we spend on negative thought. Try this exercise; I found it revealing. Sit down with a piece of paper and a pencil close at hand and close your eyes. For ten minutes, think only positive thoughts. Each time you slip in a negative thought, open your eyes and make a little tally mark on the paper. Then, close your eyes and continue. If you worry about a negative thought coming in, that counts as a negative thought, because worry is negative. At the end of ten minutes (you will, of course know this because you have set a timer,) open your eyes and count your tally marks. Now, multiply that number by six, because that is the number of ten minute segments in an hour. Multiply that number by the number of waking hours in your average day. You may even need a calculator! That is the number of negative thoughts you have each day. Pretty scary, isn't it? And that's when you were trying NOT to have them.

If you want to see something REALLY scary, try a twist on the previous exercise. This time, close your eyes and concentrate very hard on something about which you feel great fear and anxiety. Try to envision it in detail and then take note of what is happening to your body and your mind. What do you feel? Sweaty palms, heart palpitations, stomach flutters? Negative thoughts take a toll on body and spirit; but only if we allow them to control us. We CAN choose not to let them into our lives. If they start to sneak in, sometimes we need to physically boot them out.

I am a great believer in attaching physical gestures to thoughts. Maybe I am strange, but when I notice an unhealthy thought trying to crash into the neighborhood of my brain cells, I physically shake my head to get rid of it. For some reason, this makes me feel as if I have literally shaken it out of my brain. I also tend to lose earrings this way, but it's worth it to me.

I have a friend who is the C.E.O. of a huge corporation. He, of course, has many responsibilities and worries, which he had been taking home with him. As a matter of fact, he used to wear those pressures like chains. When his constant fretting threatened his marriage, he adopted my "gesture" theory. He says that people look at him as if he has gone around the bend, but each day before he leaves the office, he writes down all of his current concerns and physically locks them in his desk drawer. He then backs out of the office and orders the problems to stay behind. According to him and his wife, it has made all the difference in the world, because he has given himself permission to leave his worries at the office and has changed his behavior pattern.

Sometimes, it is easier to simply move away from the negative, and not concentrate so intently on moving toward the positive. If we focus on breaking negative patterns and refuse to step back into that circle of despair, we are taking steps in the right direction. An elderly friend of mine once shared with me her theory about longevity. She said, "If we would all quit worrying about being happy all of the time and just get on with the business of living, we'd be better off, because if we're not busy living, we're dying!"

I learned something else from her, too. She happened to be 97 years old at the time, so I figured she would be a likely person to share secrets of long life. When I asked her to what she attributed her many years of reasonably good health, she replied by naming the three most important aspects of her existence. She called them the three "senses" and they are as follows: Sense of self; feeling comfortable with who and what you are. If you aren't comfortable, fix what needs to be fixed. Sense of community; the best way to come out of your blue mood is to come out of yourself and give to someone else. Sense of humor; you don't have any sense if you don't have a sense of humor!

Our attitude affects how we deal with others and how they perceive and relate to us. Our attitude is also contagious; would we want someone to catch ours?

Moving Away From Negativity

Sometimes it is necessary to have a strategy to defuse negativity. By recognizing a negative cycle, we can then take tangible steps to reverse it.

 * **SET ASIDE A TIME FOR NEGATIVITY:** For instance, allot a half-hour in the evening. Do not allow yourself to "jump the gun" and think any negative thoughts before your designated time. (The anticipation will be half the fun.) Choose a time and a place where you will not be interrupted and for that period, allow yourself to focus on any and all problems and negative thoughts. Stick to your schedule and do not let anything stand in the way. Now, really be negative! Worry about anything and everything because remember that to worry is to enjoy a crisis before it has even occurred. You may as well get a head start. Use this time to replay scenes of anger, frustration, rejection, and any other less than positive events. Every day, decrease your worry session by five minutes. That means you will have to worry harder and faster to get it all in, but don't allow yourself to fudge on the time or use any other part of the day to "negatize." As you gradually decrease your neg-a-time, you will find that you are more selective about the negative thoughts you are entertaining. You will notice that you are worrying less and enjoying it more! Although this exercise is being presented in a tongue in cheek manner, it does have value. We can learn to control our negative thoughts and by limiting the time that we allow ourselves to embrace them, we

condition ourselves to realize they aren't necessary. It also allows us to view our concerns in a humorous light. I tried this exercise, and during my fourth session, I suddenly broke into laughter right in the middle of a first class worry, because I caught sight of myself in the mirror, hunched over with my face contorted in a scowl, trying so hard to keep up the mood. The truth was, at that moment, my mind was wandering and I really was bored with worrying. It was then that I realized how nonproductive negativity really is and how much of my life was being wasted on it.

* WRITE YOUR NEGATIVE THOUGHTS: Lock yourself in a room where you will not be disturbed and be prepared to write non-stop until you run out of negative thoughts. Write your fears, your problems, your worries, your feelings of guilt, your resentments, the names of the people who anger you; everything imaginable that stands in the way of your complete and total sense of peace. Write without pausing, just letting those toad-like thoughts pour out onto the paper. Now, next to each little pearl of poison, write what you get out of it. I mean, does feeling guilty give you a sense of atonement? Does feeling resentful make you feel like a martyr? Does holding onto anger make you feel self-righteous? You get the idea. You will probably find yourself feeling a bit sheepish when you put your feelings on paper and have a chance to look at the big picture. If you still feel the negative feelings are justified, you probably don't really want to break the habit. But I'm betting that you'll gain a clear understanding of your priorities. When you have exhausted yourself and your reservoir of negativity, take the paper and destroy it. Don't just throw it away; burn it, shred it, throw darts at it…anything that will completely wipe away what you have written. Now, take a deep breath and let those feelings go. You have tangibly cleansed yourself of your worst thoughts, now release them emotionally, as well. You have just de-negatized yourself. Congratulations.

* SURROUND YOURSELF WITH "POSITIVITY:" Positivity is not a word. Neither is "negatize" or "neg-a-time," which were used in the previous exercises, but they should be words, and they are now my words. You may use them as well, if you wish. Anyway, now that you have taken steps away from negativity, you must surround yourself with the healing white light of positivity. Tuck yourself away in a private place and focus your thoughts on the good things in your life. These don't have to be spectacular, although if you've just won the lottery, that would qualify. Just concentrate on the everyday flow of your life…think about your family and the laughter that you share. Think about the fact that you made it through another day with no more than one or two major catastrophes. There are many miracles that occur each day, which we often overlook because we have become insensitive to them.

Now, visualize yourself in a place of total peace and tranquility. It can be an actual place that you enjoy or a fantasyland. Some people feel the safest in places of their childhood; this might be the case for you. Let your imagination carry you until you hear the sounds, smell the scents, and feel the textures of your "comfort zone." Breathe deeply and release any residual feelings of tension. Allow yourself to float weightlessly, bathed in the white light of well being. Now, just hang there for a while. That's all...just enjoy that feeling and allow yourself to be enveloped in it. Remember that it shouldn't be necessary to strive for happiness; that will come on its own when we move away from the negative.

* GIVE YOURSELF PERMISSION TO BE HAPPY: Oddly enough, sometimes when we move away from the negative, we find ourselves in the middle of a void; a vast emptiness where the "bad stuff" used to be. We become so used to feeling anxious and miserable, we're not quite sure how to fill that spot once we move away from it. Sound strange? Sure, but that's the way our minds sometimes work. We are creatures of habit, and if we have been habitually negative, we need to give ourselves a kick in the pants in the other direction. We need to give ourselves permission to feel good.

Remember those dreaded trolls that were mentioned in the previous chapter? They are always there to convince us that we are not worthy of happiness or success or peace or anything positive. When we start to believe this, we make excuses not to be happy! At times, I have even let my trolls sell me on the idea that if my life is going too well, trouble must be on the horizon because things are too good to be true and will certainly come to a screeching halt! I can recall several times when I actually sabotaged myself and stood in the way of my own success because I allowed my negative trolls to control my mind.

Any negative emotion that you are supporting and nourishing with your time and energy is draining to you and is a burden which will eventually cause your back to bend. When you finally allow yourself to lay down your burden, for goodness sake...don't pick it up again!!! Sometimes in my Attitude Adjustment workshops we end the session by writing our "burdens" on paper and putting them into balloons which we then fill with helium. There is something very therapeutic about taking those burden balloons and letting them go straight up and out of our lives! Every time I do this, I feel a sense of peace as I send my woes into the atmosphere and regain (at least temporarily) control of my thoughts.

I used to love the old television sci-fi series, *The Outer Limits*. At the beginning of each program, wavy lines appeared on the screen and a voice instructed us that we no longer had control over our television sets and it would be useless to attempt to operate the dials. For the next hour, we allowed ourselves to be drawn into the strange and eerie world of aliens, psychic phenomena and other scary stuff. Eventually, of course, we were allowed to regain control of our televisions and our minds. Sometimes, I am reminded of that show when some negative force, like worry, fear, guilt, etc. creeps into my brain. I can almost hear that voice telling me that I am now losing control of my emotions, and I should not attempt to "operate the dials."

I have come to realize that I don't always have control over what happens in my life, but what I do have the ability to control is how I allow the circumstances to affect me. So in real life, I don't have to turn myself over to any unknown force…I can operate my dials anytime I please!

CHECK YOUR BATTERIES

We all have habits that energize us; the ones that keep us going and going and going…Unfortunately, we also have habits that drain us and keep us from operating at full speed. If we can identify those behavior patterns that suck out all our get-up-and-go, both emotionally and physically, we can take steps to replace them with positive, energizing thoughts and activities. Sometimes it is just a matter of taking the time to list and evaluate our behavior patterns. The following exercises may help to put things into perspective.

LIST THE HABITS THAT

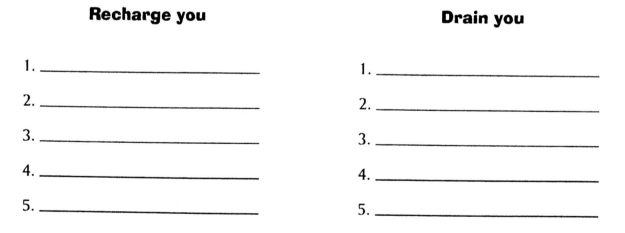

Recharge you

1. _____
2. _____
3. _____
4. _____
5. _____

Drain you

1. _____
2. _____
3. _____
4. _____
5. _____

PRINT THE LETTERS OF YOUR NAME. FOR EACH LETTER, CHOOSE AN ENPOWERING WORD THAT BEGINS WITH THAT LETTER. FOR INSTANCE: I AM JOE. I AM JOYFUL, OPTIMISTIC, AND ENTHUSIASTIC

Lesson Eight:
Laughter and Attitude Adjustment

If we don't master negativity, it will master us. We must always remember that we are more important than our problems. Negativity is a toxin and sometimes we need to "detox" our brain.

If we set our mental channel on POSITIVE and leave it there, we will be amazed at our capabilities. As Henry Ford said, "If you think you can do a thing or think you can't do a thing, you're right."

I have found it helpful to create my own good humor mantras. I repeat them over and over to myself, because I am a hard nut to crack when it comes to breaking negative habits. To change focus, I sometimes chant something like "I will not be intimidated by reality." Occasionally, I get really creative and cute with "Oh joy, oh rapture; another glorious day to capture," but most of the time, the best I can muster is "It could be worse!"

Negativity becomes a way of life. Sometimes we need to talk to ourselves like we would talk to a friend. We wouldn't tell a friend that they deserve to feel lousy. We'd encourage them to "kick" the negative habit. We need to be our own best friend.

"If I have lost every other friend on earth, I shall have at least one friend left and that friend shall be down inside me." –Abraham Lincoln

"Human beings can alter their lives by altering their attitudes of mind."–William James

"Humor is a means of obtaining pleasure in spite of the distressing affects that interfere with it."– Sigmund Freud

"To hate and to fear is to be psychologically ill. It is, in fact, the consuming illness of our time."— H.A. Overstreet

"Do what you can, with what you have, with where you are."–Theodore Roosevelt

*"Puff, puff, chug, chug," went the Little Blue Engine. "I think I can, I think I can,
I think I can, I think I can." – "The Little Engine that Could."*

Life On The Laugh Track

At times, we all feel somewhat "humorally challenged." Humor skills don't always come naturally…sometimes we need to develop and sharpen them and practice humor habits.

People who are not used to delivering quips or making jokes may feel that they just aren't funny…but humor is not about being funny. Humor is the ability to counter-act possible negative situations by using the "light touch."

I delight in reflecting on the funny things I have seen in some not so funny places. I am constantly amazed by the way some people are able to find humor to help them cope with unpleasant situations. I was impressed by the creativity of a resident of a retirement community, who walked with a cane and found it difficult to stand in the buffet line in the dining room. Rather than to complain about the inconvenience, she got her message across in another way. One day, she approached the dining room manager and requested that there be two separate lines…one for those who were mobile and another for those who walked with crutches and canes and needed more assistance. Before her meeting with the manager, this clever lady had fashioned two cardboard signs to be used to designate the appropriate buffet lines. One sign said CANE and the other said ABLE. The manager, delighted with the idea, had the signs recreated in wood and they are there to this day.

Playful thinking can become a habit, which will get you through many difficult situations without blowing your top. When you find it hard to come up with a logical solution for a problem, try flipping your mental channel over to "imagination" and play with the challenge. By doing this, you can reframe the problem…undo what you don't like and redo it! Let off some steam and you'll probably hit upon a solution.

In his book, "The Healing Power of Humor," Allen Klein tells of an office manager who repeatedly submitted a budget, only to have the executive director send it back with the note "Reduce It!!" When the frustrated manager had nipped and tucked and cut it as much as possible, she decided to play with the problem and took the budget to the copying machine where she hit the "reduce" button and shrunk it down to a fraction of its original size, after which she gave it once again to her boss, along with a memo stating that her budget was reduced as much as possible. The executive director later appeared at her door, laughing. With budget in hand, he acknowledged that he had gotten the point and appreciated the good-natured way in which she had sent the message.

It is amazing how one little break in a negative pattern can lighten up even the darkest mood. I have a friend who has hit upon a little exercise to defuse potential arguments with her husband. Whenever things start to feel a little tense, before she says anything she'll later regret, she pops on a big rubber clown nose that she keeps close at hand. She calls it her "Nip It In The Bud Nose" because it always stops fights before they start. I guess it would be hard to argue as or with Bozo...so rather than raise their voices, she and her spouse end up laughing and the spat is forgotten. I remember one time, when her in-laws were visiting...she wore that nose for a solid week.

Making humor a habit is a matter of surrounding ourselves with reminders not to take ourselves too seriously. I have a sign over my make-up mirror that says: EAT A TOAD FIRST THING IN THE MORNING...NOTHING WORSE CAN HAPPEN TO YOU FOR THE REST OF THE DAY. This helps me to put things into proper perspective...although I'm not quite sure just why.

"If you can find humor in anything, you can survive it."– Bill Cosby

Seventeen Silly Yet Satisfying Stress Busters

☺ If you are an American, you will spend almost six months of your life waiting at red lights. Instead of fuming about the terribly taxing traffic troubles, carry a bottle of bubbles in your car and have fun seeing how many you can blow before the light changes. It will occupy you and entertain the other drivers.

☺ On a sheet of toilet paper, write a list of all the things that are annoying you... then flush it!

☺ Put on some upbeat music and shimmy, shake, twist, and shout for three minutes. This will definitely revitalize you. Your co-workers will get a kick out of it too.

☺ Take time to play with a child. Jump rope; play tag or hopscotch... anything you haven't done for a while. Play for play's sake...forget about the competition angle.

☺ Surround yourself with things that make you feel good. Have toys and humor props in your work area. Carry anti-stress props with you; bubbles, yo-yos, etc.

☺ Keep close at hand, a picture of yourself laughing! Refer to it often and visualize happiness. The picture will remind you that there is more to your life than your worries.

☺ Finger paint. This is one of the most liberating feelings you can experience! Don't be afraid to be messy and let it squish between your fingers...that's the fun part! If you have to be clean, at least get yourself some crayons and a good coloring book. Don't even worry about staying in the lines, just express yourself.

☺ Stand in front of the mirror and make goofy faces. You may want to refrain from doing this in a public place.

☺ Write uplifting thoughts on sticky-tabs and stick them everywhere...on your phone, in your purse or pocket, on your steering wheel. Use them as "thought conditioners."

☺ When you're angry and ready to explode, drop everything and sing a silly song or dance a little jig. Guaranteed: you'll forget your anger and entertain your co-workers.

☺ Hang a sign over your mirror that says, "DO NOT TAKE THIS PERSON SERIOUSLY!"

☺ Set aside at least fifteen minutes of quiet time each day. Tuck yourself away in a place where you can be undisturbed and empty your mind of every negative thought so you can fill it up again with positive affirmations. This could prove to be a challenge, especially if you have a family who is always demanding a piece of you. Remember, you cannot help others if you do not help yourself.

☺ Make up a "Humor Pantry," a collection of stories, puzzles, games, pictures, etc; anything to make yourself laugh in times of stress. Keep it where it is readily accessible.

☺ Vent your frustrations. No one can deny a frustrating feeling...you need to deal with the problem and move on. Keep a squishy rubber toy to squeeze the daylights out of, or a toy drum you can beat in times of anger. Letting it out will keep it from backing up inside you and creating future problems.

☺ Do something nice for someone else. It's a sure-fire way to feel better about yourself.

☺ Send a letter to yourself in which you write nice things about you.

☺ Keep a "Joy Journal" of things and thoughts that bring you happiness. Do the same thing with a "Humor Diary" (funny things you see and hear.)

☺ End each day by reading or listening to something pleasant... NOT THE NEWS! Make the last thing you do before sleep, a positive experience.

Laugh 'til the Cows Come Home!

WRITE A DICTIONARY DEFINITION OF YOU:

_____ n. 1. _____
Your name
_____
_____
_____
_____
_____
_____
_____
_____
_____
_____
_____
_____
_____

Write a definition of you as you would like to be:

_____ n. 1. _____
Your name
_____
_____
_____
_____
_____
_____
_____
_____
_____
_____
_____
_____

Adjust Your Attitude

Music Soothes The Savage Beasties

"Music hath charms to soothe the savage breast; to soften rocks or bend a knotted oak."

These beautiful words from "The Mourning Bride" by William Congreve, create a passionate image of the power of music.

I am convinced that every person in this world is bilingual. I know this to be true because there are two languages, which are the universal communicators and understood by all…they are laughter, and music.

I stand steadfastly by my belief that music is the ultimate mood-altering drug. Composers know exactly how they want people to feel while listening to their music, and if they are successful in their endeavors, most of us have no choice but to be enveloped in the precise mood the notes were written to induce.

Listening to music conjures diverse emotions, captures memories of long ago, and carries us to faraway places in our minds.

Consider the role that music plays in our everyday lives. Hollywood uses it to the fullest to place us in just the right mood to succumb to the full effect of what's happening on the screen. Take away the eerie, pulse racing, terror-building strains accompanying the monster approaching its victim, and it's just not the same. We can close our eyes in fear of what we're seeing on the screen, but if we still hear the music, what we conjure up in our own minds is really twice as frightening. Music creates a feeling, and anticipation. It completes the effect.

Advertising firms are particularly aware of the importance of music in conveying their messages. Who among us, has not sat in front of our television and wept as we "celebrated the moments of our lives" with film, phone, and coffee companies who crept into our souls on the wings of strings playing heart rending melodies. I've bought plane tickets to go visit my mother because the airline commercial song so touched me. Of course, my mother lives less than a mile from me, so the tickets were probably unnecessary.

The point is that music enhances, enriches and empowers us. It can make us feel jubilant, animated and uplifted, or it can mellow, sadden or relax us. Imagine the power we can derive from this mood inducing, non-toxic drug!

When I am conducting Attitude Adjustment workshops, a segment is directed toward inducing a mental state through music. People are often amazed at what they learn about how they are affected. Try it yourself…if you are feeling particularly blue, put on the happiest, peppiest music you can find and just let your body go with the feeling. Dance, jump around, sing; anything that the music calls you to do. Chances are, if you give in to the music, you'll be dancing away from those blues before you know it.

Remember those old Hollywood musicals in which people found answers to their problems by singing? The thought is really not so silly! It is virtually impossible to frown and feel miserable when you are singing at the top of your lungs (unless you are a blues singer.) It doesn't matter if you can't carry a recognizable tune…just the physical conditions that are created when you're crooning are enough to improve your spirits. When you sing, you must take deep breaths and have good posture; this alone will make you feel better.

The next time you are alone in your car, stuck in traffic, turn up the radio, throw back your head and howl. Add some gestures and gyrations for good measure (assuming you are still paying attention to your driving) and watch what happens. You'll feel energized and the other drivers will be entertained.

I know of an office in which the staff relieves stress by singing to each other. Instead of merely asking someone to pass the stapler, the request is put to music. The effect is hilarious. Of course, they are careful to do this at appropriate times.

The theme of this book is "moving away from negativity" and utilizing music is one of the most effective methods toward this end. Make a cassette tape of your favorite upbeat songs, comedy routines, or just sounds of laughter. Keep your "Happy Tape" close at hand for a quick fix in times of stress. So "Don't Worry, Be Happy," try "Singing' In The Rain," and remember to "Whistle While You Work."

Lesson Nine: Laughter and Creativity

Laughter is rich soil for the seeds of creativity. In order to unleash our creative minds, we must first knock down the roadblocks of negative thinking.

We need to give ourselves permission to let our imaginations soar and a laugh-conditioned mind is the best launching pad for these creative thoughts.

"Imagination is more important than knowledge."– Einstein

"Many of the problems associated with creativity are in the form of emotional blocks within one's self."– John E. Arnold

"You can't depend on your judgment when your imagination is out of focus."– Mark Twain

"My special place. It's a place no amount of hurt and anger can deface. I put things back together there. It all falls right in place—in my special place."– Joani Mitchell

Have a Mental Block? Turn It Into a Building Block

Even the most creative of people sometimes experience blocks which stand in the way of solving challenges or completing tasks. Who among us, has not locked ourselves in our office, resolved to work, only to end up making paper clip chains or paper airplanes? Just me? I don't think so!!

Here are some ideas, adaptable to all ages and occasions, designed to unclog the pipes and let the flood of creativity flow:

FIND A MONSTER: Think of something that you want to do even less than the project that has you stumped. Clean out the catbox, pay bills…anything that you aren't particularly fond of doing. This is not to say that there is anything strange about you if you ENJOY cleaning the catbox and paying bills, however…oh well I never mind. Anyway, just the thought of a worse task might be enough to start your project engine.

BREAK IT DOWN INTO BITE SIZED PIECES: When you're feeling overwhelmed, remember that an impossible task can be more easily tackled when it is in manageable segments. Define each challenge; assemble all of the information, think of possible solutions, take a break; rest and relax, and then evaluate which idea is best. Don't underestimate the importance of taking a break when you feel completely saturated with a problem and have reached an impasse. Drop it altogether, go for a walk or go to a movie and consciously forget about it, because what is really going to happen is that your subconscious mind will take over. It's amazing how many times an answer to a problem will pop into your head when you're right in the middle of thinking about something else. This happened to me once, when my husband and I were trying to remember the names of the Seven Dwarfs. This seemed to be critical at the time. Anyway, try as we would, that seventh name just wouldn't come to us. It wasn't until hours later, when I had been sound asleep for a while, that it hit me. So excited was I, that I jumped up in bed, hit my poor husband with a pillow while chanting "Dopey, Dopey, Dopey!" I believe that he had totally forgotten about those Dwarfs and thought I was passing judgment on his character. Oh well, maybe that isn't the best illustration, but you get the point. Take a break when you need one.

DAYDREAM: We are often taught that daydreaming is unproductive and therefore, unacceptable. Most adults do not cultivate this habit and we usually do not encourage our children to daydream either. Yet, much creative thinking springs from reverie and quiet moods that on the surface seem to be divorced from reality. Carl Jung wrote, "The dynamic principle of fantasy is play, which belongs also to the child, and appears to be inconsistent with the principle of serious work. But without this playing with fantasy, no creative work has ever yet come to birth." Go Carl! Of course, all things in moderation, etc. etc. etc., but if you can daydream without feeling guilty, you'll find it a valuable tool in breaking down those mental blocks. Daydreaming and temporarily removing yourself from the tasks at hand will fan those fires of imagination, which will in turn bring forth the answers to your challenge. When your imagination is allowed to soar, as the inimitable Dr. Seuss wrote, "Oh, the thinks you can think!"

ESTABLISH A POSITIVE MIND-SET: To achieve a creative attitude, assert this simple statement: "I am creative." When you affirm your own creative ability, you will minimize debilitating self-doubts and create a positive mind-set that will be an important aspect of the creative attitude. To become more creative, think of yourself as a creative person. You will become relaxed and less rigid in your thinking. Once you begin to believe what you're telling yourself, your awareness and perceptions will become more acute and you will find yourself more sublimely in tune with the creative you.

YOUR PERSONAL AND PRIVATE "FUNNY ROOM"

Close your eyes and imagine a room that is entirely your own; equipped, decorated and furnished any way you please. It is a private place, to which you can go when you want to feel completely relaxed and entertained. In this room, you store mementos of past experiences which have given you moments of laughter and joy.

Take your time and imagine funny pictures, cartoons, props, etc., which decorate your room. When you are completely relaxed and comfortable in your room; shout out the first word that comes into mind - it can be totally ridiculous (it probably will be.) From now on - when things get tough and you need to briefly retire into your funny room, repeat your trigger word to transport yourself back into your special place where you'll find peace and good thoughts.

Everybody's gotta have their "Laughin' Place."– B'rer Fox

Life Offers A Plethora Of Puzzles To Ponder. Stretch Your Mind And Jump Start Your Imagination While Considering...

☺ Why are there interstate highways in Hawaii?

☺ Where does fat go when you lose it?

☺ Do you need a silencer if you are going to shoot a mime?

☺ If the 7-11 markets are open 24 hours a day, 365 days a year, why are there locks on the doors?

☺ If nothing ever sticks to Teflon, how do they make Teflon stick to the pan?

☺ Why do we drive on parkways and park on driveways?

☺ Why is it that when you transport something by car it's called a shipment, but when you transport something by ship it's called cargo?

☺ Why is the word brassiere singular and the word panties plural?

☺ How does the guy who drives the snowplow get to work in the morning?

☺ You know how most packages say "Open Here"...what happens if you open it somewhere else?

☺ You know that little indestructible black box that is used on planes...why don't they make the whole plane out of the same substance?

☺ What kind of sheep gives steel wool?

Meet Your Monster

Imagine the thing that is bothering you the most.
Give it a personality and a face!

Create Your Own Captions

Lesson Ten: Laughter and Play

We adults sometimes forget the value of play. Play and creative silliness energize and empower us and allow us to view challenges in a more positive manner.

Sometime between the ages of diapers and gray hair, we lose the valuable childlike quality of "wonder." We become cynical, "sophisticated," and stuffy! We need to stop occasionally and ask ourselves: How would the child we used to be evaluate the adult we've become?

Try to keep in touch with the elf in yoursELF and follow these instructions daily:

☺ Keep in contact with the child within

☺ PLAY

☺ Allow yourself a little "creative nonsense"

☺ PLAY

☺ Put no boundaries on your imagination

☺ PLAY

☺ Take several daily "joy breaks"

☺ PLAY

☺ Start a toy collection

☺ PLAY

There is a difference in being ChildISH and being ChildLIKE. There's POWER in PLAY.

"Children have a remarkable talent for not taking the adult world with the kind of respect we are so confident it ought to be given. They refuse to appreciate the gravity of our monumental concerns, while we forget that if we were to become more like children, our concerns might not be as monumental."–Conrad Hyers

---

"I am absolutely certain that being happy is what keeps you young; and laughter helps you to do that. You have to find out what makes you happy and just hope that it's legal."–Phyllis Diller

---

Find The Elf In Yourself

Anyone who spends any time around children knows that they give themselves permission to have fun. When they think something is funny, everyone around them knows it. Children are constantly erupting in giggles and their laughter is contagious!

We first laugh at about two months of age. By the time we are four years old, we are laughing at the rate of about one laugh every five minutes. Then, as we mature, an amazing thing happens. Along the path to adulthood, we become too sophisticated to laugh so indiscriminately. If we were to continue on with the same fancy-free attitude, other people might look down their noses at us, maybe even consider us "childish." Oh horror!

So, in order to fit nicely into the "grown-up" mold, we monitor our laughter and silliness and make sure that we only display it at "appropriate" times, for instance, when we are intoxicated.

Because we have all read the Grown-Up Handbook, we know that not only should we cease to participate in creative silliness when we hit adulthood, but we also recognize the importance of sending a clear message to the children in our lives. We must serve as role models in negativity, lest the poor little ones get the mistaken impression that growing up is a desirable thing to do!

So, we glare at them when they act silly, chastise them for "goofing off," and smirk as we sarcastically dish out the news that they'd better have fun now, because when they grow up, they'll learn what life is really about!! Our very favorite thing to do to our children is to demand that they "act their age." This is particularly effective when addressing a six-year-old who is giggling and acting like a...six year old.

Isn't it amazing that our kids ever want to grow up? I know so many adults who are bitterly unhappy and unfulfilled because they still buy into the theory that play is only for children.

GROWN-UPS OF THE WORLD UNITE! Break loose from the surly bonds of INHIBITION, the oppressor; lift up your heads and howl! Step away from your desk and wiggle, squiggle, and do a little jig! Dislodge that stick that has been stuck you know where, and lighten up! Remember what it feels like to PLAY, just for the sake of playing, with no competition involved.

Go buy yourself a bottle of bubbles to keep in your desk drawer or in your car. The next time you're stuck in traffic, instead of grumbling about it, whip out the bubbles and fill your car with them. Not only is this a great stress breaker, but it thoroughly entertains other drivers, particularly if you try to catch the bubbles on your nose. It's a real crowd pleaser.

Surround yourself with things that make you feel good. Ladies, this does not mean Mel Gibson. Create for yourself, an environment that is conducive to creativity and fun. Children are famous for carrying toys and little gadgets around with them in their pockets. They bring their favorite things to school and generally keep their happy memories close at hand. Adults tend to keep their mementos locked away in trunks and their pictures closed in albums. Try keeping "touchstones" with you so that in times of stress, you can focus on memories of less stressful times. Decorate with cartoons, funny pictures, bright colors, and anything that cheers you. Don't be concerned about whether it complements the decor.

Remember to play. If you have forgotten how, fear not…it comes back to you. In other words, find the ELF in yoursELF. Don't worry about your dignity; there is a difference in being childISH and childLIKE. Aim for childLIKE.

The problem with grown-ups is that we tend to separate work and play. We feel that if we are having a good time while we are working, we are not taking our job seriously. Actually, play is an integral part of the thinking process; it breaks down mental barriers and opens the rivers of creativity.

People of all ages will be more productive if they are enjoying what they are doing. Take several play breaks during the day and never be fooled into thinking that being silly is the same as being stupid. Some of us can do both equally well, but then, we're not talking about me right now. Anyway the word **silly** comes from the old English word **saelig**, meaning completely happy. People wished this for their loved ones, because total health includes happiness and emotional balance.

A recent study conducted at a university consisted of dividing a class of graduate students into two groups. Both groups were prepared to take a rather difficult exam, but before the test was administered, the students were told that there had been a mix-up in the scheduling of the testing rooms, which would result in a slight delay. The groups were sent to separate rooms to await the commencement of the exam. One group was put into a room with a television, which was tuned to a news program. They spent their time watching video footage of recent news stories, consisting of the usual…wars, robberies, death, and destruction. The other group was led into a room usually occupied by children in a daycare program. It was full of toys; electric trains, yo-yos, bubble blowers; a selection of various playthings. Of course, it was hard to resist picking up these toys, so while waiting to take the test, these students played. Both groups were then given the exam and the results were very revealing. The students who had been subjected to the news program before taking the test scored 30% lower than those who had played. Why? Because negativity permeates and infects our very souls. Laughter and play, on the other hand, fills us with a sense of well being and positive attitude. Negativity clogs our brains and weighs us down, whereas laughter frees our thoughts and sends a message of success.

We could well take a clue from this study. We want the best for ourselves and of course, hope for success in the future. People are more receptive to learning in a positive environment. Laughter allows us to disassociate and detach ourselves from a threatening situation and choose an attitude of success.

There is nothing juvenile about laughter and play. As a matter of fact, maturity comes with the ability to remain childlike. Play is a sign of great wisdom and insight into good mental health. It's not so much that playing lays aside the tensions of life; it's just that it moves within those tensions and creates comic relief.

I hope you will take the challenge and let yourself know that you care about yourself by getting in touch with that child you used to be and start associating with him/her again. You may find you've become so afraid of playing your child won't want to hang around with you, but give yourself a chance and your child will show you what to do.

Above all, keep high above you the banner of PLAY. Remember how empowering and healthy it is. As the great actress Ethel Barrymore once said, "You grow up the day you have your first good laugh--at yourself!"

The Right To Play

I recently read about a survey in which a group of one hundred people were asked if they were generally happy with their lives. The magazine article reported that 22.5 of the people questioned stated that they felt their lives to be satisfactory.

What does that mean? When I read the results, I must admit I was taken aback by the statistic 22.5. The .5 is what confuses me. Does it refer to a person who is half-happy or does it suggest that one of the individuals polled is very short?

All kidding aside, I was saddened by the number of people who appeared to be dissatisfied and unhappy with their existence. What really distressed me, however, were the results of the next question asked: "How many times a week do you take time to play?" A whopping 88 out of 100 answered "none." It didn't take long to understand why the majority were unhappy campers!

We are all born into this world with a beautiful golden spirit and a genuine sense of wonder. Every day of a child's life includes a serious dose of play. Then we become "groan"-ups and spend our time being concerned with "important stuff." Granted, we might find ourselves losing favor with the boss if we toss a football in the office or make paper airplanes out of file folders, but that's no reason to ignore our need for a little mental "recess" every now and then.

After reading about the aforementioned survey, I challenged a group of friends to join me in making TILTD lists; (Things I Like To Do.) The idea was to come up with lists of activities that nourished us and gave us a sense of joy about being alive. Most of us wrote fast and furiously for about 20 seconds and then just sat there, pencils in hand, with a blank stare. The results were very enlightening. The reason that most of us had trouble thinking of anything was because it had been a long time since we had done anything that we liked to do. Apparently, we had all contracted Terminal Seriousness.

We began to compare notes and discuss how far astray we had roamed from the play ethic in which we had believed so strongly as kids. We had forgotten how to imagine and wonder and just do something for the fun of it. With all of today's technology and emphasis on efficiency and time management, life-sustaining joy is being seriously threatened!

It seems that as adults, we will only allow ourselves to play if competition is involved. I have a friend who "enjoys" playing tennis. His idea of enjoyment differs from mine, because when he loses a game, he screams and beats his racket on the ground. If tennis gave me that much "enjoyment," I'd just as soon use my racket for a spaghetti strainer!

You might find some value in starting your own TILTD list. It may only consist of three items at first, but that's okay. The important part is allowing yourself to make time in your busy schedule to do the things on your list. It is helpful to actually write them on your calendar or daily planner, because you will be more likely to play if you have given yourself permission and logged it in. Schedule yourself some recess time every day. Take a walk, read a book, talk to your dog, or just "zone out" and think of nothing, if that is what you like to do. There are no rules; just play for the sake of playing. If you're like me, you'll find that your TILTD list will grow and you will magically find time you didn't know you had, to participate in life-giving fun.

There are no prizes at the end of life for terminal seriousness. As a matter of fact, I would be willing to bet that very few people leave this earth wishing they had struggled more and laughed less. On the contrary, nurturing joy in our hearts enhances our lives and stimulates our productivity, creativity, and effectiveness.

On the next page, you will find a wonderful certificate, which you should cut out, frame and hang on your wall. It is a Certificate of the Right to Play and by signing it, you will be giving yourself permission to respect yourself enough to take the first steps toward a joyful, peaceful, well-deserved happy life!

I end this section with a philosophical quote from a kindergarten student: "If you don't play and have fun, your brain grows small." So there!!

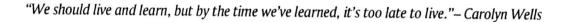

*"A person without a sense of humor is like a wagon without springs
—jolted by every pebble in the road."*–Henry Ward Beecher

"We should live and learn, but by the time we've learned, it's too late to live."– Carolyn Wells

Certificate

of the Right to Play and Not be "Groan"-Up

By this certificate know ye that

_____

is a lifetime member in good standing in the
Hang Onto the Elf in YoursELF Society and is
hereby and forever entitled to the following:

Scratch when and where it itches; walk in the rain without a hat;
jump in puddles, even while wearing dressy shoes; smell
flowers; go barefoot; play hopscotch, jacks, marbles, and any
other game just for fun, not for competition; fly a kite; blow
bubbles; act silly; dig in the dirt; wear colorful clothes; color in
coloring books; read children's books; buy toys to keep at the
office; sing on the way to work; stay up late; play on swings;
climb trees; do nothing, look at the stars; find shapes in the
clouds; daydream; eat without worry about calories;
tell stories; smile at people; learn something new just
for fun; dance; try a new hair-do; refuse to worry
about tomorrow; decorate with things that don't
necessarily match, just because they're neat; play
with a child; visit a friend; learn to say "no" to
demanding people; and practice things that bring
more happiness, health, fun, and laughter to life.

Furthermore, the above-named certificate holder
is officially entitled to pull his or her panties out of
a bunch and laugh and play for the health of it.

Things I Like To Do

Write down the things you like to do; the things that make you feel good and happy and carefree. As you're writing, make a mental note of the last time you participated in these things. Is it because you don't have the time? Grown-ups don't do these things? People will think you're silly? Promise yourself that you will do at least one of these things per week for the next six months. You are worth it. Remember, you are responsible for your own happiness.

_____

_____

_____

_____

_____

_____

_____

_____

_____

_____

_____

_____

_____

_____

_____

Lesson Eleven: Looking for Laughs in All the Right Places

If you don't think there is anything funny in your life, you're just not looking! Take a look around you…the world is your comedy club!

The most important humor skill is the ability to see the humor around you and appreciate it for what it is. There is humor in almost every situation. It may be disguised, but it is there.

Have some fun recalling your most embarrassing experience, your first date, or first day on the job. Can you remember your biggest "goof" or the funniest sign you've ever seen?

A sense of humor is much deeper than laughter. It is finding fun in everyday experiences.

"Life literally abounds in comedy if you just look around you."– Mel Brooks

---

"If I keep a green bough in my heart, a singing bird will come to it."–Chinese proverb

---

Mirth is like a flash of lightning that breaks through a gloom of clouds and glitters for a moment, cheerfulness keeps up a kind of daylight in the mind, and fills it with a steady and perpetual serenity."–Joseph Addison

---

Humor is an affirmation of dignity; a declaration of man's superiority to all that befalls him."– Romain Gary

---

"When we lose our sense of humor, we lose our footing." –McMurphy in "One Flew Over the Cuckoo's Nest"

The World As a Laugh Lab

There is no comedy show; no entertainment of any kind that can compare with the humor that appears regularly in our everyday lives. Comedy is everywhere, and if we aren't seeing it, we just aren't looking!

In this age of technology, it is more important than ever for us to maintain a connection with other people and remember the value of non-technical communication. We need to develop humor skills and be aware of all the fun that surrounds us. We all deserve this!

A while ago, I started the practice of carrying a little notebook with me wherever I went, in which to jot down the things I saw that made me laugh or smile. I began doing this six months ago and I am now in my fourth notebook. I have learned that everyday people doing everyday things are infinitely more entertaining than anything any movie company could ever produce!

Consider for instance, the sign outside the church, which stated the following:

SUNDAY'S SERMON: WHAT IS HELL REALLY LIKE?
Come in and hear our choir sing

Or, how about this one, also by a church:

WHAT REALLY IRRITATES GOD?
Pastor Robert Scott

One of my all time sign favorites was spotted on the marquis of a casino. Obviously, the owners were attempting to advertise that they provided lounge entertainment as well as offering patrons a chance to play a betting game. But the way the sign was worded required a double take.

TONIGHT ONLY - JENNY MYERS
CRAPS IN LOUNGE

This one conjured up a mental image of people dragging themselves into work.

LANDALE BORING COMPANY RESTRICTED ENTRANCE
BORING EMPLOYEES ONLY

OR HOW ABOUT
The signs that have missing or jumbled letters.

MARRIAGE COUNSELING
DR. R. STORM
THE RAPIST

CARLTON HOTEL
If you're going to have an affair—have it here!

Perhaps "event" would have been a wiser choice.

HOLLY STREET HOTEL
Come Stay With Us
We Have Cheap Rats

"Say What?"

Everyone at one time or another, becomes a victim of "Foot in Mouth Disease." Who hasn't been caught with their tongue twisted or their brain disconnected for a brief moment. I, personally feel embarrassed each time I replay, in my mind, one of my finest hours, while addressing a church conference. Intending to elaborate on the Twenty-third Psalm, I clearly blurted out that the Lord is indeed our Shoving Leopard. (Originally meant to be Loving Shepherd.) Fortunately, most of us aren't in the public eye, and don't have our every word recorded for posterity. Consider the plight of those in the limelight, for they shall forever be remembered for such gems as:

"The similarities between me and my father are different." (Dale Berra, Yogi Berra's son)

"I move, Mr. Chairman, that all fire extinguishers be examined ten days before every fire." (City councilman during a debate)

"For seven and a half years I've worked alongside President Reagan. We've had triumphs. Made some mistakes. We've had some sex...uh...setbacks." (George Bush)

"I believe we are on an irreversible trend toward more freedom and democracy. But that could change." (Vice President Dan Quayle)

"I've never had major knee surgery on any other part of my body." (Winston Bennett, basketball forward)

"Did you get a good look at my face when I stole your purse?" (An accused thief who undertook his own defense at his trial)

"I apologize for lying to you...I promise I won't deceive you except in matters of this sort." (Spiro T. Agnew, to reporters)

"Sure, it's going to kill a lot of people, but they may be dying of something else anyway." (Member of a Texas pesticide review board, speaking about chlordane)

"I want to hear it so quiet we can hear a mouse dropping." (Hollywood director)

"The best cure for insomnia is to get a lot of sleep." (S. I. Hayakawa)

"Brooks Robinson is not a fast man, but his arms and legs move very quickly." (Curt Gowdy, sports announcer)

"This portion of 'Women on the Run' is brought to you by Phillips' Milk of Magnesia."
(Radio announcer in the 1950s)

"When a great many people are unable to find work, unemployment results." (Calvin Coolidge)

"China is a big country, inhabited by many Chinese." (Charles De Gaulle)

Anytime you need a laugh, you need only to hop into your car and drive. Inevitably, you will come upon a sign, posted, no doubt, in all seriousness, guaranteed to make you smile:

MEMBERS AND NON-MEMBERS ONLY. (Sign posted outside a disco club in Mexico.)

PLEASE FEEL FREE TO TAKE ADVANTAGE OF THE HOUSEMAID AT ANY TIME (Sign in a hotel room in Japan.)

NOTICE: ALL WATER AND GAS HAS RECENTLY BEEN PASSED BY THE HOTEL MANAGER (Posted in a hotel lobby in Mexico City.)

FREE COFFEE TO ALL IN CAR WITH GAS (Sign at roadside gas station.)
*Note: This leads one to wonder how one must prove who, in the car, has the gas.

FOLLOW THE ARROWS TO THE SOLAR SYSTEM AND RESTROOMS (Sign in the N.Y. Hayden Planetarium.)

WHEN THE MACHINE STOPS, REMOVE ALL YOUR CLOTHING (Posted in a laundromat.)
*Note: This has the potential to create an unpleasant sight.

DROP YOUR PANTS HERE (At a dry-cleaners.)
*Note: Maybe the same people hang out here as at the laundromat.

COME VISIT OUR DRIVE THROUGH SALAD BAR (On a fast food restaurant marquis.)
*Note: Picture this!

Warnings that are issued for our own good fill us with a true sense of security and trust in the responsible companies:

BEWARE! TO TOUCH THESE WIRES IS INSTANT DEATH. ANYONE FOUND DOING SO WILL BE PROSECUTED (On a sign at a railroad station.)

For more of these little beauties, you may want to check out -
The 776 Stupidest Things Ever Said *by Ross & Kathy Petras.*

Adjust Your Attitude

BEWARE! TO TOUCH THESE WIRES IS INSTANT DEATH. ANYONE FOUND DOING SO WILL BE PROSECUTED (On a sign at a railroad station.)

EXPOSURE TO DIOXIN IS USUALLY NOT DISABLING BUT MAY BE FATAL. (Warning issued by a Chemical Company.)

WARNING: DO NOT ATTEMPT TO DRIVE CAR WITH SUN SHIELD IN PLACE. (On windshield sun blocker.)

CAUTION: DO NOT SPRAY INTO EYES. (On the label of breath freshener spray.) *Note: eye halitosis <u>could</u> become a serious problem.

BLOOPER DU JOUR

Restaurant menus are often rich sources of blooper humor. Consider the following, lifted from actual menus in restaurants around the country:

Today's Specials: Beef...$6.50   Chicken...$5.50   Children...$3.50

Comment: "I'll have my child medium rare, please."

Special Today: Chapped Liver

Adults are cordially invited to wait for seating in our cocktail lounge. Ladies are not to have children on the bar.

All of our meals are home cooked. We are especially proud of our Dreaded Veal Cutlet.

We will bar-b-que your children right in front of you on our giant open pit.

Mother Martha's Sunday Special: Braised Beef Tips on Needles

Humor in the News

Believe it or not, your local newspaper is a never-ending source of entertainment. Between the articles describing doom, death, destruction and despair...(in detail) are hidden some choice tidbits which are not designed to make you laugh, but by their goofy wording or dangling participles, induce snickers. Here are some questionably worded ads and headlines, which deserve a second look:

☺ BURNS FURNITURE is your hometown furniture store. Why go elsewhere to be cheated when you can come here?

☺ JOB OPPORTUNITY: Wanted: man to work in dynamite factory. Must be willing to travel.

☺ THREE STATES HIT BY BLIZZARD--ONE IS MISSING.

☺ LAWYER TO OFFER POOR FREE ADVICE

☺ For Sale: Antique desk for ladies, with thick legs and large drawers.

☺ Bring your car to us for service and you'll never go anywhere again!

☺ Huge Baby Sale - New and Used

☺ FOR SALE: Pot bellied pig. Eats anything. Is especially fond of children.

☺ South Florida Headline - "Illegal Aliens Cut In Half By New Law"

☺ South Carolina Headline - "Police Begin Campaign To Run Down Jaywalkers"

☺ New York Headlines - "Strange Robbery In Police Station-All Toilets Are Stolen-Cops Have Nothing To Go On!"

Humor in the Pews

Reinhold Nieburh said, "Humor is a prelude to faith and laughter is the beginning of prayer." I like that. I also like what a former kindergarten student of mine said: "Smiling is turning the corners of your mouth up toward God."

I believe God has a sense of humor and I believe that we have been given the glorious gift of laughter to enhance our lives and better appreciate the world in which we live. I don't think it's any mistake that infants begin to smile and laugh at about two months of age. There is nothing more innocent and flawless than babies; they are about as close to God as you can get. And laughter is one of their first forms of communication.

We look to our places of worship for comfort and peace, but often we also find laughter. After all, the Lord loves a merry heart! Consider the following from assorted church and synagogue bulletins and signs:

On Wednesday, the Ladies Literary Society will meet:
Mrs. Johnson will sing "Put Me in My Little Bed," accompanied by the pastor.

Thursday, at 5:00 p.m. there will be a meeting of the Little Mother's Club.
All women wishing to become Little Mothers will please meet the minister in his study.

Our choir is seeking new members. If you like to sin, we want you.

Don't let worry kill you off...let the church help.

Remember in prayer, those who are sick of our church and community.

The ladies of the church have cast off clothing of every kind and they may be seen in the church basement on Friday afternoon.

For those of you who have children and don't know it, we have a nursery downstairs.

This afternoon, there will be a meeting in the south and north ends of the church. Children will be baptized at both ends.

On Sunday, a special collection will be taken to defray the expense of the carpet. All those wishing to do something on the carpet, please come forward and get a piece of paper.

The rosebud this morning is for James Michael Townsend, the sin of Reverend and Mrs.Townsend.

We shall all meet in the sanctuary at 9:00 a.m. to prepare for a day of prayer and farting.

Note: Oops... perhaps "fasting" would be more appropriate!

The sign outside the church listed sermon titles as well as times for the services. One Sunday it read:

I 1:00 a.m. Jesus Walks on Water

7:00 p.m. Searching for Jesus

"Angels can fly because they take themselves lightly."– G.K. Chesterton

Lesson Twelve: Humor and Aging

All of us have one thing in common: like it or not, we are all aging. From the moment we are born, we're constantly getting older. Sounds profound, doesn't it? Even though common sense tells us that we are in a constant state of aging, we all still think we can fight it! It's amazing that we believe that by coloring our hair and soaking in "Oil of Delay," we have control over the sands of time.

Well, we can fight it, but it would sure be easier just to allow ourselves to "go with the flow" and sail on the crest of the "age wave," using laughter as our sailboat. The trick is to keep sailing and avoid getting stuck in the sands of time!

The best defense we have against having our ship "dry docked," is to laugh and play through every day. Humor is an ideal way to transfer anxiety about aging into pleasure. George Burns was a master at this, as is evident in his classic line, "I'm glad to be here…but, at my age, I'm glad to be anywhere." The day we stop playing is the day we start growing old and losing the magic.

"Death is not the greatest loss in life. The greatest loss is what dies inside us while we live."–Norman Cousins

"How to tell if your life on earth is through? If you're alive, it isn't."–Richard Bach

"I don't stop laughing because I get older, I get older because I stop laughing."– J. Coldwell

"How old would you be if you didn't know how old you was?"–Satchel Paige

---

My mother always used to say: "The older you get, the better you get, unless you're a banana."
–Betty White as Rose Nylund in the T.V. show "The Golden Girls"

When Your Fountain Of Youth Becomes Clogged With the Sands of Time

I am now a grandmother. Even as I write the words, they seem somewhat incomprehensible to me. But as I look upon the sweet faces of my grandchildren, I know that it is indeed real.

Grandmotherhood really gives one a sense of power! I suddenly feel as if I have earned my place in the annals of parenthood and progressed into the higher ranks.

Things and people that used to intimidate me are now put into proper perspective, and I feel as if I can do anything! I am grandma...hear me roar.

I realize, of course, that I am getting older and my physique is changing. I still have everything that I had before; it's just a little lower now. The sands of time are shifting. I have made a few changes in my life to accommodate my mutating body. Now, if I am standing, I no longer bend over to speak to someone sitting, lest my entire face droop into their lap. I now must lie flat on the floor while zipping my jeans. This seems to do the trick, although when I stand up, my neck looks bigger. I guess the fat has to go somewhere. I have bought a gallon jug of Oil of Delay and use it faithfully. If a little is good, a lot is better. Soon I will be marinating in it.

I am not, however, afraid of aging, because there is nothing wrong with getting older. Sure, the songs of my wild youth are now being used in advertising jingles and elevator music. Okay, maybe I have the beginnings of an identity crisis. I'm just not sure where to go with it. I can't identify my identity. All I know is, I'm somewhere between birth and death.

I am too old for rock concerts, but too young for rocking chairs. I am too old for hot dates, but too young for hot flashes. Some of the fashion statements and slang language of my youth is back in style again and I feel as if I am caught in a giant time warp. For instance, when I was sixteen, I wore mini-skirts and labeled things that I liked "cool." Now, sixteen-year old girls still wear mini-skirts and things are once again "cool," but no one thinks that a middle-aged mother is "cool" when she wears mini-skirts and says that things are "cool." See what I mean? I am caught somewhere in the limbo zone between hot pants and sensible shoes. I'd like to think of myself and my circle of friends as being like the cool group of people in the movie "The Big Chill;" people who are passing into their next decades with grace and class. Unfortunately, sometimes, when we all get together, it is less like "The Big Chill" and more like "Night Of The Living Dead."

I am a victim of society's labels. And now, some genius along the way has determined that I am an honorary member of an elitist group called the Baby Boomers. What on earth is a baby boomer anyway? It sounds like a bouncing infant toy. The other day, I read a headline which stated that corporate baby boomers are on the rise. I formed a mental picture of a group of men and women sitting around a conference table in high chairs, wearing power ties and diapers. This article went on to inform us that the baby boomers were not going to accept aging. That's quite a stand they're taking! I was encouraged to learn that I now have the ability to simply refuse my next birthday as easily as I can turn down another helping of broccoli.

Unfortunately, we sometimes tend to view life in a rear view mirror…comparing present situations to the way things used to be. We fuss and fume and worry that life is passing us by. When we do this, we get stuck in quicksand…our fountain of youth becomes clogged with the sands of time!

I have a friend who is eighty-nine years young. She is the most delightful, happy-go-lucky person I know; always smiling, with a twinkle in her eye, even though she is confined to her bed a large part of the time.

One day, I asked her how she dealt with getting older; how she kept the sands of time from clogging up HER fountain of youth. When I asked her, she threw her head back and laughed, with that glorious, contagious, merry chuckle that is her style. With her laugh, she was answering my question. Youth is not a chronological age; it is a state of mind. Everyone has to choose the way they perceive things, and we all have the choice to take things too seriously, or swallow them with a healthy dose of laughter.

I have decided that in general, life just doesn't work out right, and that's what makes it so funny. Things go haywire and people do too. Every situation has the potential for humor, because life is funny. Therefore, it follows that the longer we live, the more experiences we will have which will give us the opportunity to laugh. The older we become, the richer in laughter we will be. I know that many jokes are made about aging and most of us are afraid of losing our shape and getting lines on our faces. But although our skin may wrinkle, our spirits never will; not if we condition them regularly with laughter, because laughter is exercise for the soul.

And so, my beautiful and wise friend taught me that laughter is the plunger that will unclog my fountain of youth. That's what it's all about…finding humor in every day experiences. Any of us could probably take a week out of our life and extract enough material for a stand-up comedy routine, because today's mishaps make tomorrow's funny stories.

I will try to never again allow my fountain of youth to be clogged with the sands of time. I have too many things to do. I want to experience life to its fullest and do everything, except maybe wear a bikini in public and eat liver.

I have learned that we all have a tremendous capacity for humor, but if we don't use it, we tend to lose it. I have found great truth in the words, "Laugh and the world laughs with you; cry, and your mascara runs."

How To Know If You Are Not Aging Gracefully

☺ When you ask the lady at the cosmetic counter if she has any make-up tips for you and she answers, "Use a lot."

☺ When a neighbor child asks her mother, in your presence, why you have air bags under your eyes.

☺ When you are able to trace the rivers of the United States, using your legs as the map.

☺ When you need a bi-focal windshield on your car.

☺ When you realize that if you are to ever again have a perky chest, you will need to use jumper cables.

☺ When you go for a physical and end up with a doctor that is not as old as your tube of eyeliner.

☺ When the most dangerous part of sunbathing is no longer skin damage, but being seen in public in a swimsuit.

☺ When your idea of living dangerously is to skip flossing for one night.

☺ When your husband buys you a lifetime gift certificate for a complete make-over...with a money back guarantee.

☺ When you actually consider using Preparation H to shrink the bags under your eyes.

☺ When "going for the burn" means experiencing a hot flash.

The Challenge of Finding Your Inner Self When You Can't Even Find Your Car Keys

About the time my forty-fifth birthday rolled around, the truth blazed before me like the candles on my cake. I needed to reevaluate myself inside and out to find out just who I was and where I was going. Society was telling me that I was on my way to being over the hill, so I felt I owed it to myself to see just what was on the other side.

A counselor friend of mine suggested a self-awareness retreat in the high mountain country, where "The earth meets the sky and your soul learns to fly." This sounded just weird enough to be intriguing, so I packed a bag and told my husband to eat whatever wasn't moving in the refrigerator, because I was going off to find myself.

"It's not surprising that you lost yourself," he replied, "your sense of direction is terrible." He was right. I can get lost in a phone booth.

"That's not what I mean and you know it!" I snarled, "I'm going off to find what I'm all about; to find the inner me."

"You make it sound like you've left your internal organs laying around somewhere."

"I'm leaving," I said, "But I'll be back in a few days with the new me."

"I'll look forward to seeing both of you," he answered.

At the retreat site, I stood with twenty other women who were there to devote two days to uncovering the mysteries of our existence. We were greeted by a wonderfully wise looking woman wearing a turban. I was thrilled. I knew she must be a truly mystical person who would be able to guide me in my search for my special purpose.

She smiled and said, "Please forgive the turban, but I just got soaked in the rain and I can't do a thing with my hair." My bubble was burst. She was no mystical sage. She just had hair that looked like wet spaghetti in the rain, like the rest of us.

We were all assigned to rustic cabins. I thought this was pretty primitive, since my idea of roughing it had always been a motel with no remote control for the television.

I asked the turban lady where I could plug in my curling iron and hair dryer. She informed me that I would not need such things because I was there to meet my true inner self. I tried to explain that I did not want to meet myself with hair that looked like squirrel fuzz. She was not amused.

After dinner, we were to get to know our cabin mates, as we were to be each other's guides in our quests for finding our inner beauty. I wasn't sure that I could handle the responsibility. I couldn't even find my car in the grocery store parking lot. How could I be expected to guide someone to their inner being? What if I lost them along the way? Panic began to nibble at my self-confidence.

My cabin mate turned out to be a woman by the name of Carrissa, who was at this retreat to see if she was as perfect as she thought she was. Everything about her was strong and capable. She made me feel about as confident as a rabbit at a fox family reunion. Carrissa the Competent was a take-charge kind of person. To hear her talk, she always saved the day. While jogging by a school one day, she single-handedly talked a sniper down from the rooftop, thereby saving a playground full of children from certain death. She never perspired, had bad breath, or got those raccoon eyes from smeared mascara. She knew how to cure most common diseases by using natural herbs and minerals, she typed her crossword puzzles, and she could probably have cooked a minute steak in thirty seconds. Carrissa explained that she was not married because she could find no man who could match her good looks, strength, and intelligence. She was anxious to find a husband and start a family. I thought to myself, that any man who tried to convince her of his redeeming qualities, would have a better chance of dancing on the head of a pin. As for Carrissa's maternal instincts, I just couldn't picture her wiping strained peas off the walls or fishing in a toilet to retrieve a rubber snake that had been flushed by a toddler. I considered suggesting that she start out with a pet or a houseplant to get the hang of motherhood.

When it was my turn to introduce myself to the group, I was expected to explain what I hoped to accomplish over the weekend. How could I explain what I really didn't know myself. The truth was that my hemlines kept getting lower and lower because my knees were getting lower and lower. My legs were beginning to look like relief maps showing the rivers of the world, and I needed panty hose the thickness of inner tubes. I was beginning to feel the passage of time. The songs of my youth were being used as jingles on toilet paper commercials. Life was speeding past me, out of control.

I mumbled something about wanting to accomplish something before I became too old to remember it. I explained that I have never been one of those women who can whip up a sumptuous dinner for eight using the leftovers in her refrigerator. For one thing, I never have any leftovers. There is something in my fridge that resembles a science project, but I haven't yet mustered the courage to research its origin. Nor can I feed a family of four on $.67 a week, put together a theme party at the drop of a hat, or redecorate the office on my lunch hour, making it more efficient in air-flow and space utilization. In short, I am Martha Stewart's worst nightmare. She may be able to create festive window treatments out of worn-out dish towels, build on a room-addition to her house utilizing implements found in the typical kitchen junk drawer, and spin straw into gold, but I can't.

On top of everything, it seems like everyone else in the world is motivated to do great things. They all want to Soar With the Eagles, Swim With the Sharks, and Run With the Wolves. I've never been that motivated. I am content to Play with the Squirrels and Nap With the Cats. I had always considered the day to be successful if the kids still had all their body parts in tact and nothing alive got sucked up in the vacuum cleaner.

Carrissa listened to my rantings and volunteered that she had found true fulfillment when she went on an archaeological dig, looking for artifacts from ancient Greece. I explained to her that I had spent my whole life digging in ruins. I had cleaned up after two kids, one husband, three dogs, four cats, one fish, and a psychotic hamster. And if I wanted to see ancient "grease" I could simply look behind my stove.

We talked into the night, analyzing, sharing, and searching for our true purposes. At one point, shortly after midnight, I thought I had discovered the meaning of life, but I fell asleep before I worked out all the details.

The next morning, we met the new day, tired but secure in the knowledge that we had all found the reasons for our existence. Carrissa the Competent had found time to devise an ecological plan, which would patch the holes in the ozone layer, reverse global warming, and save the whales. She decided to throw away her checklist of husband qualifications and start dating men instead of auditioning them.

As for me, I discovered that too many Carrissas in this world would be overwhelming. Some of us have to be average. We can't all fix our own plumbing, re-tile our kitchen floors, and construct backyard greenhouses using Popsicle sticks and recycled jelly jars. I have learned to take joy in my small accomplishments, like lining my shelves with sticky contact paper and not getting it stuck in my hair. I have started to take pride in the fact that I can make my grandchildren laugh by making funny faces and talking like Bugs Bunny. I probably would have figured it all out sooner or later, even without that retreat experience. One thing I did learn on the mountaintop…you can cover a multitude of hair problems with a turban!

Surfing on the Age Wave

This aging thing is complicated. As I get older, I am becoming convinced that it sometimes gets a bad rap. I always thought that when I became a grandmother, I would pull on my support hose and sensible shoes and maybe head out to the nearest community center to enroll for a class on "Optional Bodily Functions" or perhaps "Holding Your Adult Child's Attention Through The Use Of Guilt."

Well, now I am a grandmother and what do you know...I am not finished having fun yet! Some things have changed a little; for instance my sands of time have shifted and I look a little different than I used to. But I don't believe in rear view vision. I do believe in looking toward the future. Baseball legend, Satchel Paige once said "Don't look back because something might be gaining on you." I have experienced quite a bit of "personal growth" in my backside area lately, but I don't think that's what Mr. Paige meant when he said those words. I have found that many people are uncomfortable with the thought of getting older. My friends sent me black balloons and Over The Hill cards on my last birthday. For Christmas, I received a tee-shirt on which was printed these words: "I'm a senior citizen, now give me my damn discount!"

We joke about getting older because Western society is still somewhat youth oriented. Most of us probably dread aging because through advertisements which feature pencil thin, clear skinned young humans, we have bought into the theory that youth means beauty and age does not. We nip, tuck, pluck, and suck excess skin in an attempt to defy our years. We marinate in Oil of Delay, and wash away the gray, yet deep down inside, we fear that we can run...but we cannot hide! My personal belief is that we have choices in life and how we age is one of those choices. As Gloria Steinam said when asked what "50" feels like..."A lot like "40" used to feel." Everything is relative.

The truth is that life is not linear, it is cyclic. That means that just because one phase of our life, career, etc. is finished, we're not! People in their sixth, seventh, and eighth decades are embarking on new adventures. Workers are retiring from their jobs, but not from their lives. Some are going back to school to learn new skills as they begin new careers.

I have learned that many of the ills attributed to getting older are not really due to the aging process at all, but rather to a lifetime of neglect. In other words, we spend our younger years abusing our bodies and then blame old age for the results. That reminds me of the old joke about the 99 year old man who tells his doctor, "If I'd known I was going to live this long, I'd have taken better care of myself!"

As I get older, I take great pleasure in reading and hearing about others that have achieved greatness and accomplished wonderful things in their later years. For instance, consider the following: George Bernard Shaw penned "Farfetched Fables" in his 93rd year. Galileo discovered the phases of the moon when he was 73. Louis Pasteur discovered the cure for hydrophobia in his 60s. I always have felt a special kinship with Pasteur because we both worked with molds...he, in his laboratory and I, with the bread that I forgot in the back of my cupboard. And of course, you probably will remember the great fitness guru, Jack LaLanne, who celebrated his 40th, 50th, 60th, and 70th birthdays by swimming in oceans and pulling steel boats through the water with his teeth. Personally, I prefer celebrating my special days with a few friends, eating birthday cake and opening presents…but that's just my choice.

The point is that getting older doesn't necessarily mean falling apart. The key to successful aging at any point in life is attitude. It is possible to go with the flow and sail on the crest of the age wave, using laughter as our sailboat. The trick is to keep sailing and avoid getting stuck in the sands of time. We may not be able to choose the way we die, but we certainly can choose the way we live and we can choose not to die before our body does.

Rear View Vision

How old do we have to be before we don't need laughter? Sixty-five? Eighty-one? At what age does our funny bone become brittle and disintegrate? Well, the fact is that we NEVER lose our need for humor as long as we're alive. Now, it is true that some people die when they are very young and just don't fall down. They are the walking dead…you know the ones. They roam the earth for years, picking up layers of guilt, fear, hostility, negativity, grumpiness, and anger, and wearing them like chains. Of course, these burdens weigh upon a person and choke out any signs of life. The people who choose this way of life are suffering from osteoporosis of the funny bone.

Just as we take vitamins and calcium to strengthen our other bones, our funny bones need daily doses of Vitamin H (Humor) in order to continue functioning.

Too many times, we tend to look at our lives through a rear view mirror. As we get older, our conversation is punctuated with phrases like "the way things used to be" and "when I was younger." We speak of the good old days and spend a lot of time looking backward instead of toward the future. The past is valuable because that is where we acquired our experiences and memories, which make us what we are today. But the future is where we're headed, so we may as well look where we're going! Humor is a link with the past and an affirmation of continuing life and vitality.

We are not programmed to self-destruct at any particular age. My father, a man of great wisdom and laughter, has always told me that we will live until we die. Now, that might sound pretty simplistic, but you can't argue with it. My dad is trying to make the point that when people get to a certain age, sometimes they figure that the best is over and they just waste the rest of their time waiting to die. And there are a lot of ways to die besides just physically. When we sit and mope and mourn the fact that we're not twenty years old anymore, we are slowly killing our spirits.

Sometimes, we just automatically assume that when we get older, we will have more aches and pains. Since studies show that most of the physical problems that accompany aging are not a result of the aging process, but rather from a lack of proper health care in our younger years, we lay a lot of blame on getting older, when the problems really started when we were young and careless. Old age is not a sickness and chronological age has nothing to do with our ability to have fun and enjoy life.

Two of the most fun loving people I know are in their eighties. They happen to be my parents and whenever I need cheering up, I go to them. Probably the reason that they are so positive, is because they believe whole heartedly in the power of laughter.

Humor is an attitude toward life and a willingness to accept life and ourselves with a certain light heartedness and mastery over any given situation. I remember asking my mother to name the best time period in her life. I loved her reply, "Whatever age I am at the time…that's my favorite!" What a wonderful way to live!

I had the good fortune to spend some time working in a retirement community and learning many life lessons from the residents there. Probably the most enlightening thing I discovered was that people do not become grumpy and crotchety when they get older…the ones that are crabby when they are old were crabby when they were young! On the other hand, the people who have that twinkle in their eyes and a genuine love of life are the ones who practiced good humor habits and conditioned themselves with laughter.

In working with senior centers, retirement communities and nursing homes, setting up Comedy Clinics, I have had the delightful opportunity of seeing some of the incredible ways people are still "seasoning" themselves with humor. I will never forget the old gentleman wheeling himself down the hall with a horn on his wheelchair and playing cards clicking in the spokes of the wheels! Then there was the dear lady of ninety-five who printed these words on a piece of poster board and propped it on her nightstand: "I'm not dead…I'm only sleeping!" These and others like them have a deep understanding of how laughter is a thread that winds through the tapestry of life. They know that we don't stop laughing because we grow old, we grow old because we stop laughing.

Our faces may acquire a few lines, but if we condition ourselves with laughter, our spirits will never wrinkle. As Shakespeare wrote, "With mirth and laughter let old wrinkles come."

Lesson Thirteen:
Laughter in the Workplace

Unfortunately, some people are of the opinion that if we laugh and enjoy ourselves at work, we are not taking our work seriously. Nothing could be further from the truth! It only makes sense that if we enjoy what we're doing, we will be more productive and creative and that positive energy is contagious!

According to a survey commissioned by Northwestern National Life Insurance in 1990, thirty-four percent of United States workers admitted to considering quitting their jobs due to excessive stress. Is there some kind of a law which states that we have to develop an ulcer or drop dead with a heart attack in order to prove that we're taking our job seriously? There's no glory in that!!!

How do we break that killer stress syndrome? Some people will feel comfortable wearing clown noses to work, whereas others might prefer to forego a "nose job." But everyone needs to find some form of release and humor seems to be applicable in just about every work environment.

It is true that everyone brings joy to the workplace...some, when they enter and others, when they leave...but laughter is the great equalizer. It is wise to remember that you aren't responsible for making anyone else laugh, so you can have your own private humor techniques which bring you peace and make you chuckle. People will also wonder what you're up to!

Sometimes, in order to preserve our sanity and perform at our maximum level, we need to stir up the ashes of burnout and fan the flames of fun!

"The body cannot tell the difference between what is actually happening and what you are imagining. When you consider all the negative fantasies that run through the mind each day, it's no wonder that the body stores so much tension."
–Joan Borysenko in "Minding The Body, Mending The Mind"

Get More Smileage Out of Your Staff
(co-worker, patient, student, etc.)

Humor maximizes memory
Laughter liberates learning

Humor in the Workplace can...

☺ manage conflict

☺ motivate people

☺ foster creativity

☺ relieve stress

☺ put things into perspective

☺ improve morale

☺ promote teamwork

☺ cut down on absenteeism

☺ establish positive relationships

☺ create a non-threatening environment

People with a sense of humor are...

☺ more creative

☺ less rigid

☺ receptive to new ideas

HELPFUL HINTS TO PREVENT
W•O•R•K
FROM BECOMING A 4 LETTER WORD

You don't have
to be
CRAZY
to work here...
but it helps!

"Humor and attitude make a powerful statement about a company and what it represents."–Anonymous

Office Antics

☺ Equip your office or work area with a "Joke-Jar." Everyone brings at least one joke per week to contribute.

☺ Start a humor newsletter featuring brief stories of humorous goings-on around the workplace.

☺ Make posters which reflect the spirit of humor in your office. For example: COMPLAINTS WILL BE HEARD BETWEEN 10:00 AND 10:03 AM.

☺ Adopt a secret pal program. Participants draw names from a hat and over the course of a month, anonymously provide his/her secret pal with inexpensive little trinkets, funny cards, etc. Secret pals' identities are revealed at a staff "Pal Party."

☺ Tape a long piece of butcher paper along one wall. Keep markers or crayons nearby for people to display their humorous side through art.

☺ Have everyone in the office bring in pictures of themselves as babies. Put them up on the bulletin board and let people guess who they are; (once you've seen a co-worker as a chubby little cherub, you never quite view them the same again.)

☺ Select an office "Dear Blabby." Everyone with complaint about the workplace can write to him/her for advice.

☺ Pass out a "rush job" calendar with the days numbered backwards, so you can order something on the 7th and receive it on the lst! (most effective in getting the point across to an impatient employer who wants something done "yesterday.")

☺ If there is a "community pet peeve;" something that bothers everyone (for instance, a bothersome office policy,) make a likeness of it and use it as a dart-board (in the employee lounge.)

☺ Write a soap opera using your workplace as the setting and co-workers as the stars. Let everyone take turns writing the latest episode based on the latest office activities, and turn workplace frustrations into laughter.

☺ Once a month, have an office "theme day." Example: Wild West Day - people dress in western clothes, western music is piped in, and lunch is a "Prairie Potluck."

☺ Cut out cartoons and cut off the captions. Put them on the bulletin board and have people write their own captions.

☺ In your office's break-room, lay in a supply of games, toys, puzzles, funny books, etc. Let people enjoy "recess" at break-time.

LAUGH - O - GRAMS

Spice up boring memos with your own personalized
LAUGH - O - GRAMS
(Make copies and staple them into note pads)

(WHINING!)

Read this then swallow it!

This Memo contains absolutely no
Sex *or violence . . .*
but please read it anyway.

THIS MESSAGE IS:
2 important
2 be _____
4 gotten

I DON'T WANT TO DO THIS —
SO YOU DO IT!

FROM THE DESK OF _____
(Isn't it amazing that my desk can write?)

CREATE YOUR OWN
LAUGH - 0 - GRAMS

Adjust Your Attitude

TANTRUM MAT

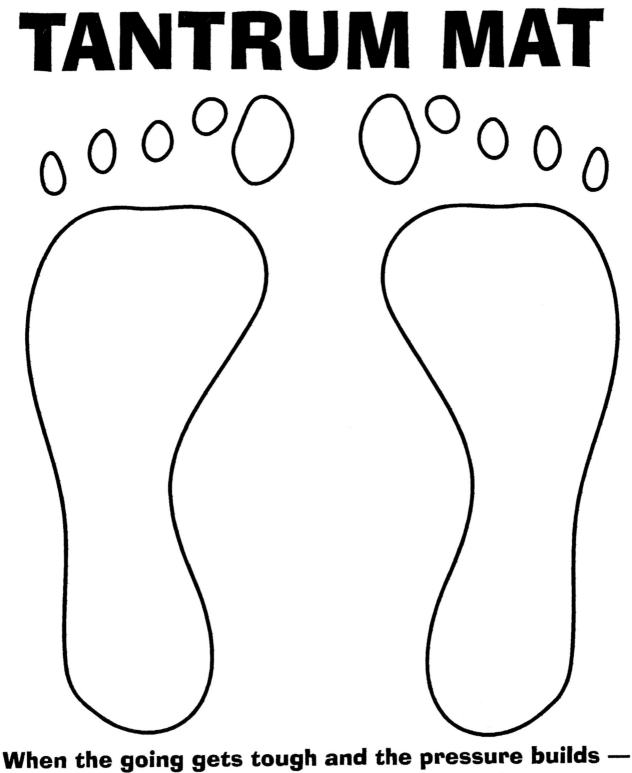

**When the going gets tough and the pressure builds —
take a few minutes to stomp your feet
and enjoy a good old-fashioned tantrum.**

Adjust Your Attitude

Lesson Fourteen: Laughter and Life Stories

Everyone's life is funny, I guarantee that there is some measure of humor in everyone's world...except maybe for the lady at the bank who has to help me untangle my checking account every month. Some of the funniest stuff on television is not Hollywood sit-coms, but rather the shows like *"America's Funniest Home Videos"* and the other programs that portray life as we can relate to it...when funny things happen to normal people doing normal things in their everyday lives.

The following is a collection of essays based on my routine existence, which always seems to go just exactly in the opposite direction of that which I plan or expect. As you will see, in some ways, my life resembles a giant practical joke. When I find out who's behind it, I'll demand an explanation.

Most of us could probably take any given week out of our life and extract enough material for a comedy routine. The problem is...it always seems funnier when it's happening to somebody else!

"Laughter is the shortest distance between two people."– Victor Borge

"An onion can make people cry, but there has never been a vegetable invented to make them laugh."–Will Rogers

Humor is a means of obtaining pleasure in spite of the distressing effects that interfere with it."–Sigmund Freud

"Laughter is like changing a baby's diaper... it doesn't change things permanently, but it makes everything okay for a while."– Michael Pritchard

---

"Show me a slightly frazzled woman with a forgotten curler in her hair and a little piece of toilet paper trailing from her shoe... and I'll know I'm looking in a mirror."– Linda Henley-Smith

---

The Truth About Men and Women

As I progress through life, I am becoming increasingly aware of one truth that I hold to be self-evident—men and women are different. Forget the popular "in-vogue"

concept that women are from Venus and men are from Mars. The truth is when it comes to some things, we're not even in the same universe!

Take shopping for instance. Most men, and I'm speaking in generalities here, hit the mall and are out again faster than a greased pig through a chute. My husband looks at things in the store window. If he doesn't see anything that he likes, he moves on. He feels that if the storeowners picked their best stuff for the window and he doesn't like anything, there's not going to be much chance that he'll like any of the other merchandise inside. I couldn't shop like that. For me, looking at everything is part of the total shopping experience. I leave no blouse untouched, no shoe untried, no price tag unturned!

The other day, we set out to shop for clothes to wear to a "black-tie" affair. To my husband, a dressy occasion is anything that requires socks. That's what was on his shopping list...socks. I was out to purchase everything that I felt was necessary to push-in, pull-up, shift, lift, separate, and hide undesirable bulges in my one and only "dressy occasion" outfit. After six hours of non-productive shopping, I decided that it would have been easier to just rent a tux and accessorize it. Men don't realize how easy they have it. You don't have to hold in your stomach while wearing a tux.

My husband is very fond of irregulars. He will pass up the other merchandise and home in on any display table that happens to hold items labeled "irregular" or "factory seconds." One day when we were shopping, we came upon a display of underwear just piled up on a table under a sign that read SLIGHTLY IRREGULAR.

My husband laughed with glee. This was right up his alley. He dove into the pile and came up with three packages of boxer shorts that were labeled "Bloopers." He was delighted. I was skeptical. How on earth could one expect to find comfort in shorts that were, by their very name, mistakes? He bought them. He wears them. He walks a little strangely now and then, but for the most part, they work.

Don't get me wrong...I am not averse to purchasing an item on sale. As a matter of fact, the less I pay for an article of clothing, the more it is worth to me. Even if I am not particularly fond of a dress, if it is on sale, it has to be good! Finding a discounted designer dress is particularly rewarding. Designers have our numbers. They know how to get us to spend large sums of money on clothing. They sew together pieces of material and make garments, which are cut extraordinarily large. The more expensive the dress, the bigger it is cut. Then they label them with size numbers that are disproportionate to the actual size of the garment. If you have enough money, you can actually find a dress out there that is labeled a size two and would fit Arnold Schwarzenneger.

Another area in which men and women differ is in their love of cars. Again, I am speaking only in generalities. I am sure there are many women out there who really care about what's under the hood. I just don't happen to be one of them. My husband loves his car and expects that it will love him back. He takes it very personally when something makes a funny rattle or a part falls off. I try to explain to him that it is a piece of machinery, but he looks wounded and whimpers, "But I treat it so well…"

He will not take the car to a car wash because it's too delicate to go through those tough brushes and violent water sprays. He hand-washes it with special cleaners and conditions it with something akin to baby lotion. My allegiance to my car goes as far as the car goes. I get in, I drive, I stop, and I get out. If something goes wrong with it, I get angry and call a tow truck to carry it out of my sight.

As a rule of thumb, men will not ask for directions. While vacationing in New York, my husband drove over the Verrazano Bridge five times, paying tolls each time, before admitting that he needed help. Finally, on the sixth pass, the man in the tollbooth gave us money. If Moses had asked for directions, he may not have had to wander for all those years.

My husband and I balance each other out when it comes to worrying. I say he's a Worry Warrior; he says he is cautious. A few weeks ago, I received an emergency call at work. My husband's breathless voice choked on the other end of the line. Sweat poured from my brow and my heart skipped a beat as my mind raced and I envisioned all sorts of tragedies that could have prompted such a call. I couldn't believe my ears as I listened to his frantic outpouring of the latest calamity…it seems as if I had used his library card and neglected to return the books that I had borrowed. Yes, it was true…I was overdue! He had just received the news via mail from the library. He calmed down only after I assured him that his reputation in the business world was in tact and he would not have to leave town to flee the library police.

Women just seem to take things in stride. Pioneer women have been known to plow a few acres, give birth to an eight-pound baby, repair a hole in the roof, and still have time to whip up a nourishing dinner…all within a day and without anesthetic. I guess it's just that women are bred to face some things that require great endurance, like pregnancy, childbirth, and bikini waxing. Most women do not have time to be sick.

I have a friend whose husband is quite the hypochondriac. The good news is that his diseases usually only last for a day, but the bad news is that he has a new one daily. She was patient with him until he read a medical book and insisted that he was going through menopause.

Laugh 'til the Cows Come Home!   123

This is all written in fun, because I really do have the utmost respect and admiration for the male species. However, I still stand by my observation that there are basic differences in the sexes. I was visiting a friend the other day who was caring for her four-year-old granddaughter. Even the youngest female recognizes the distinction between men and women. She told me, in her four-year-old wisdom, that her daddy had something her mommy didn't have...the television remote control!

The Bite of the Travel Bug is Powerful

Whenever anyone mentions travel, I begin to salivate. I can't help it...I have wanderlust. I just love going places. It doesn't matter where...far away places with strange sounding names or nearby places with ordinary sounding names. I can be ready to go in a flash. Just give me a minute to grab a toothbrush, my hair spray, and a change of clothing, and I'll race you out the door.

Travel changes with your stage in life. When you have little children you don't leave the house without a bag of diapers, several changes of clothing, (including shoes, socks, and underwear,) snack items, first aid kits, and special stuffed toys and blankets to sleep with...and that's only when you're going for an afternoon! If you intend to stay away from home for more than twenty-four hours, you needs lots more equipment.

No one who has ever taken a road trip with young ones will soon forget the experience. Spending long periods of time confined in a car with miniature people kicking the back of your seat while asking unanswerable questions, gives you a whole new perspective. I couldn't help but think about how Moses must have felt while leading the children of Israel through the desert. Can you imagine wandering for forty years with a whole gang of people asking you, "Are we there yet?" The man must have had nerves of steel.

When the children become teenagers, all that changes. Between the ages of 12 and 18, a child vacationing with his or her parents has a job to do. That job is to act bored. No natural wonder, historic monument, or breathtaking scene is worth taking off the Walkman earphones. I once accompanied four teenagers to a well-known theme park, which is operated by a famous rodent. The only time there was a glimmer of excitement was when one of them became ill on the spinning teacup ride. The other three seemed to think that was worth the whole trip.

When the nest emptied, vacation time meant just the two of us. I'll never forget the first vacation my husband and I took without the children. My husband decided that rather than straying far from home in search of vacation paradises, we should stay in our own state, and see the sights of Arizona that we natives often overlook. This sounded like a good idea; I had heard of the many luxury resorts that grace our top tourist spots and I really did think it would be fun to see some Arizona scenery.

And so, it was with great pleasure that I stopped by the travel agency the next day, and picked up a handful of brochures advertising well-known Arizona attractions and resort accommodations. Yes, indeed, this was a fine idea that my beloved had generated. I could picture myself relaxing in one of those big hotel sunken bathtubs and then wrapping up in a fluffy, oversized towel, while sipping a cool drink on the veranda of my posh resort hotel suite, which of course, would overlook whatever canyon, waterfall, or desert mountain we decided to visit. Truly caught in the spirit, I even stopped into a cute little shop called Desert Duds and bought a few outfits for the trip. I was truly the Arizona woman…bedecked in khaki colored culottes and matching sandals.

When I heard my husband at the front door, I rushed to greet him, arms full of hotel literature. I could hardly wait to tell him that I really had embraced the Arizona spirit, and what better way to see the state than from the terrace of a five star hotel!

The moment I saw him, I knew that something was terribly out of kilter. He too had been shopping with our Arizona adventure in mind, but from the look of his purchases, his adventure was going to be a lot different from mine. Excitedly, he turned his bag upside down and out toppled some of the oddest looking items I had ever seen. He proudly displayed a gadget and with the swift speed of a ninja, whipped it around, converting it into fifty different tools; knives, forks, spoons, can openers, scissors, shoehorns, screwdrivers and a thing that removed facial hair. That one gadget looked like it could be used to do everything, from peeling potatoes to performing an appendectomy. He had bought pots, pans, plates, cups, and cans. There were lanterns and lights and things for bug bites. And everything could be folded down into tiny little bundles, which would fit into the backpack that he was now unfolding and hanging over his shoulders. I watched as he adjusted the bag so that it fit right between his shoulder blades, giving him the appearance of a large turtle.

He beamed at me and proudly announced, "I thought we'd go camping…it's the only true way to taste the flavor of Arizona."

"I don't need to taste my state," I replied, "I can enjoy it using my other senses."

He began his obviously well rehearsed speech. "I don't want to fly anywhere this year," he said. "The last time we flew, our luggage had different travel plans than we did." I winced when he said that because I vividly recalled standing at the luggage carousel with one hundred thirty-five other people, hoping to retrieve our bags. When the carousel began to turn, we all waited and watched, expectantly. For five minutes, we all stood staring at an empty luggage carousel, while the conveyor belts moved nothing along. Finally, one lone box had come tumbling down the chute. It was clearly marked, LIVE SPECIMEN, HANDLE WITH CARE. The box had no lid, and was empty. Around and around it rode, the lone occupant of the carousel. One hundred thirty-six people stood and watched, emotionless. We knew that our luggage was not going to come. At least this time there was an explanation. Obviously, whatever live specimen had been in that box had gotten out in the cargo section and had eaten all of the baggage.

Our bags eventually caught up with us, but not in time. We had been the only people at my cousin's wedding wearing Bermuda shorts, tee-shirts and sneakers.

Later that night, when I awoke to find him asleep in the recliner, wearing his pajamas, hiking boots, and backpack, I realized just how important this camping thing was to my husband. I mellowed a bit and suggested a compromise. We would stay in a luxury resort, but he could cook our meals over an open fire on the terrace. We would forego the elevator and hike up the stairs to our suite. He didn't go for it. And so it was, that I learned it is possible to live for five days without benefit of a hot bath, television, or a curling iron. I learned that when you're camping, nobody cares if your hair looks like wet squirrel fuzz and you have no make-up.

As I lay underneath the stars, I contemplated the concept that a year on Earth is shorter than a year on some other planets. Therefore, I theorized, if I lived on Pluto, for instance, I'd be much younger now. Then, I calculated my age in dog years and figured that I'd be better off living **on** Pluto, the planet, than **as** Pluto, the dog.

I also took home several other useful revelations. First, while roughing it in the forests, in the absence of indoor plumbing, it often becomes necessary to utilize nature's restroom; the area behind a tree. One would be well advised to thoroughly examine the vegetation in the area, as poison ivy in a place you can't scratch in public, is not pleasant and is most unattractive.

Secondly, if there are two inhabitants in your sleeping bag and the one that is not you has more legs than you do, evacuate the sleeping bag immediately until the second party has vacated.

Adjust Your Attitude

Most importantly, I realized that life is a lot like oatmeal that you cook over a campfire. If you stir it up and keep it warm, it's delicious and fun to taste, but if you let it sit and get cold, it turns lumpy and nobody wants it.

Air Travel… The Skies Are Only Pretending to Be Friendly

They say that time flies. Well, not on an airplane, it doesn't. As a matter of fact, for me, time on a plane drags like a snail on Valium.

It begins in the airport. Who in the world ever came up with the brilliant idea of calling the plane station a "terminal?" This word does not exactly conjure up positive feelings.

Passing through the security checkpoint where you beep if you're wearing metal, is always an experience worth having. I particularly enjoy traveling with my friend, Anna, who has metal pins in her knee. She always sets off the alarm. Anna knows this is going to happen, and she looks forward to choosing the line with the youngest, most attractive male security guard, because she knows she's going to be frisked with the hand radar gun.

I can't help but wonder about those metal detectors. I've seen a 6' 8", 300 pound, hairy, wild-eyed man with tattoos on his tongue and chains draped around every part of his body, pass through unchecked, while four armed guards pounce on me because my hair pins set off the alarm.

Once you board the plane, it's always a challenge to find a place in the overhead bin for your carry-on luggage. Now, the term "carry-on" can be deceptive, because it was originally coined to describe small bags in which travelers carried a few basic items that might be needed during the flight. Nowadays, people have wised up, and seasoned travelers carry everything with them that they will need for their entire trip. This is because they know there is a good chance they may not be reunited with the luggage that they so trustingly surrendered at the check-in counter.

The phenomenon of disappearing luggage is one of the great mysteries of the universe. Even though they put it in the cargo section of the very same plane in which you are sitting, and even though you can look out your window and see your bags being loaded…apparently some molecular dissipation occurs during the flight, and your baggage often does not arrive at the same place at the same time as you do. Go figure! I'm waiting for the next photo transmission from space to reveal that the rings of Saturn are, in reality, comprised of lost airline luggage. As a result of "missing suitcase phobia," most passengers lug carry-on bags, which are the size of steamer trunks. I've seen people board planes with computers, power saws, and furniture.

The first thing of which all fliers must be aware is that all carry-on items which you carefully stow in the overhead bins, will always be flattened by another passenger's heavier item, which will have been carefully stowed on top of yours. I have come to know and accept the fact that I will always leave a plane with a straw hat which has been flattened into a beret by a golf bag full of irons, or a one-hundred pound portable copying machine.

Finding your seat and getting situated is another interesting event. No matter how full the plane; even if the people at the check-in desk have told you that it's an oversold flight, you always hang on to the hope that the seat next to you will remain vacant, giving you some elbowroom. Of course, this can never be. As a matter of fact, I happen to believe that it is my destiny to be eternally seated next to the first place winner in the World's Most Annoying Person competition. I believe that it is a punishment for transgressions of my youth. On my last flight, I listened for five hours to a man with every medical problem in the books, and some that hadn't been discovered yet. This guy was a charter member of Hypochondriac's Anonymous. After hearing about seventy-five illnesses, complete with symptoms, I wished that he had remained anonymous to me.

In an attempt to change the subject, I picked up a magazine and opened up to an article on astronomy. "Look," I began, "It says here that they have discovered a new asteroid belt."

"No kidding?" he exclaimed, "I hadn't heard that. Where can I get one? My asteroids hurt so bad sometimes that I have to sit on a little rubber doughnut. I could sure use a belt for support!"

No matter where I'm flying, the same family always sits behind me. This unit consists of a mother with a voice shrill enough to remove rust from pipes; a father, who has just lunched on a garlic, onion, and horseradish sandwich, and insists on leaning forward to breathe down my neck; a toddler who has the kicking power of a Kung Fu kangaroo; and a very cranky baby. The airline keeps this family on staff so that when I check in for my flight, they can page them and seat them right behind me. In times of war, the government uses this family to drag secrets out of enemy spies.

Once you are seated on the plane, the pre-take-off festivities begin. These include the instructional speech by the flight attendants. In these speeches, they impart pearls of wisdom which are designed to prepare the passengers for any possible and unexpected adventures. For instance, we are told that in the unlikely event of a change in cabin pressure, the oxygen masks will drop down from the overhead compartments. We are instructed to wear these masks until oxygen is no longer necessary. I always wonder at what point in time, will oxygen not be necessary for those of us who breathe with lungs?

We are warned not to go into the lavatories, tamper with the smoke alarms, and try to sneak a cigarette. This seems to be an unnecessary warning, since it would be virtually impossible to smoke in there and keep it a secret anyway. There aren't many places for the smoke to go. You certainly can't roll down the window and air the place out!

Next, we hear from the pilot and I can never understand him. I have always suspected that before the pilot turns on his microphone to welcome us to the friendly skies, he has the flight attendant bring him a handful of marbles, which he places in his mouth before he speaks. That way, he allows the passengers to be creative and imagine what he is saying. I am never really sure if he is telling us our estimated arrival time, advising us that he is leaving the plane for a moment to have his pants pressed, or suggesting that we make our final peace and grab onto the nearest thing that looks like it will float.

I trust the pilots to do whatever they need to do, as long as they stay in the general vicinity of the cockpit. It always makes me a little edgy when I see a man in a captain's suit strolling up and down the aisles greeting people like a politician.

On my last flight, Captain Cal, as he had introduced himself, was out in the plane chatting with passengers like he was the host of a flying cocktail party.

"I can see that you are wearing a uniform with little tassels on your shoulders," I said.

"That's right, M'am," he grinned.

"Well, unless you are a theater usher on vacation, shouldn't you be in the cockpit?" I asked.

I can never afford to fly first class, and I'm not really sure what goes on in there. All I know is that everyone enters the plane through the same doors, only some of us continue down the aisle to the back section of the craft and others stop and sit in the first seats. Everything seems pretty much the same in both sections until the plane takes off. Then, all of the sudden, the flight attendants jump up and whip those curtains shut to make a divider between the first class and the rest of us.

Immediately after those curtains close, we begin to hear the tinkling sounds of clinking wine glasses and smell exotic aromas, which drift through the curtains and into the noses of we, who are in the peanut gallery. Many times, I have sat, cradling my plastic container of cheese spread and cracker crumbs, while imagining the first class passengers whirling on a dance floor to a live orchestra, and taking turns at the buffet table.

If it's a long flight, you are often treated to a movie. On my last coast-to-coast trip, the first class passengers were shown a full-length feature film in cinemascope. Those of us in coach, saw slides from the flight attendant's last family vacation to the Grand Canyon. Actually, they were quite nice.

Upon landing, we hear the familiar words of warning, that we are to remain seated with our seat belts securely fastened, our seat backs in an upright position, and our tray tables folded up, until we have come to a complete stop. Not a "sort of" stop, or an "almost" stop, but a complete stop. Of course, only the pilot really knows when we have completely stopped, because he's the one with the brakes. Meanwhile, we passengers are hopping up and down like little bobbins, waiting for our flight attendants to nod their heads, indicating that it's alright for us to unfold our cramped bodies and stand up. Then, comes the fun part...opening the overhead bins, allowing articles which have shifted during the flight, to come plummeting down on our heads.

I'm sure the Wright brothers had no idea what a can of worms they were opening up, when they first decided to soar into the wild blue yonder. I sometimes complain about airplane travel, but there's no denying...it's the only way to fly!

In God We Trust... In Family We Don't

My children always have had a sadistic streak running through them. There is something in them that makes them delight in seeing the woman who nursed them through chicken pox, scraped knees, and acne, traipse through a department store with toilet paper stuck on her shoe.

As a matter of fact, my husband is no better. I can't count on any of them to keep me from making a fool of myself in public. If you can't depend on your own family to tell you that you are wearing as much lipstick on your teeth as you have on your lips, who can you depend on?

Once, a few years ago, my husband offered to take me out to dinner and dancing; indeed an historical event to be chronicled for all time. I was light hearted and happy as a prom queen as we swirled and whirled on the dance floor. At one point, we twirled past an air conditioning vent and I felt an unusually cold blast of air on my backside. I reached down to smooth the back of my dress, only there was no back of my dress to smooth, as it was neatly tucked inside my panty hose. My face felt as hot as my bottom was cold. I snatched my husband off the dance floor and ducked into a corner to rearrange my clothes.

"How long has my backside been on display?" I hissed at him.

"Since you came back from the ladies' room about fifteen minutes and two dances ago," he answered. "Why didn't you tell me?" I snapped.

"I guess I just didn't think of it," he said, "You teach humor workshops…I thought you could use the material."

I was furious. "I guess that explains why people have been throwing money at our feet," I snarled, "I thought it was just because we were so good out on the dance floor!"

I guess I shouldn't have expected any more out of a man who wanted to wear his pajamas to a party because the invitation specified "evening clothes."

I thought I had raised my daughters better, however. I felt nothing but disgust for their sin of omission, when they let me parade up the center aisle of the church with a sticker on my rear end that said in big red letters, FRAGILE, HANDLE WITH CARE. Apparently I had bumped up against the box of glass communion cups in the church entry. The Lord loves a cheery heart, but I'm not so sure he appreciated three hundred people laughing at my derriere during the prayer.

One time when I was to be a speaker at a luncheon, I took my oldest daughter along with me. Before I stood up to speak, I leaned over to her and whispered, "Do I have anything stuck in my teeth?" She shook her head no, and I went confidently up to the podium. As soon as I opened my mouth, my daughter, in the front row, began making little gestures with her hand, pointing to her teeth. It was very distracting, and I lost my train of thought several times while trying to decipher what she was trying to say. I tried not to look at her, but once again, she caught my eye. This time she was holding a piece of broccoli from her plate with one hand and still pointing to her teeth with the other. It finally occurred to me what she was trying to say. Here I was, standing as the focal point in front of hundreds of people, and all that they were going to remember about my talk, was that I had a spear of broccoli in my teeth. As I spoke, the broccoli grew larger and larger in my mind, until I pictured myself as a human salad bar.

When I sat down, I whipped out my mirror and saw first hand, the offending vegetable. "Why didn't you tell me that I was wearing my lunch when I asked you earlier?" I whispered.

"I didn't see it then," she answered.

"Are you kidding? This broccoli is the size of a small animal; it belongs in the vegetable hall of fame! How could you not see it?"

"Don't worry, Mom," she consoled, "Probably nobody noticed it; not very many people were paying much attention to you, anyway."

I felt so much better.

Even if I couldn't count on my children or husband to look out for me in public, I could always depend on my mother. I was teaching a workshop at a women's club, and my mother was in attendance. I was wearing a silk blouse that had detachable shoulder pads. Apparently, at one point, one of the pads became dislodged and slowly worked its way off of my shoulder and onto my back. I had just finished making what I thought was a particularly brilliant point. I asked the group for questions and comments. From the back of the room, my mother's hand flew up like lightning and in her loudest moose voice she said, "Why don't you get rid of that hump on your back, you look like Quasimoto." This was not the image I had hoped to present to these ladies, seeing as how my workshop was on Dressing for Success.

Sometimes I think my loved ones set me up for embarrassment. Like the time we all went out to dinner at a restaurant that served the most delicious baked goods in town. They were famous for their world class "sticky buns." Our family had finished eating and during the course of the meal, we had asked our server for six refills of our bread basket.

Before we got up to leave, I noticed that the elderly gentleman who had been seated at the table next to ours had gotten up to leave just minutes before, and had left a full basket of those fabulous baked buns. I couldn't stand the thought of those wonderful things going to waste, so I reached over and scooped them up into my napkin and tucked them safely into my purse to take home for later. My family sat and watched me do it, and never once mentioned that the man who had occupied that table had not left the restaurant at all, but was standing around the corner making a telephone call. I had my back to him, but my two daughters were watching him watching me pilfer his food.

On my way out of the dining room, we met face to face, and in a loud booming voice, he said, "Lady, nobody has wanted my buns that badly in a long time; I hope you enjoy them."

My husband and kids sure got a lot of mileage out of that one; telling their friends about the time I grabbed another man's buns in public.

I really don't know why I continue to trust them. A few months ago, I needed to buy a dress for a fancy social affair and I let them talk me into buying a slinky little black number which fit tightly on the top, stretched down past my knees and flared out in a ruffle around the bottom. The ruffle was made out of big black feathers, and I looked like a formal feather duster, It just wasn't me; I was used to breezy, flowing things that I could wear without having to concentrate on holding everything in. This outfit was about as comfortable as creeping underwear. But my girls convinced me that it "did" something for me. Looking back on it now, I can't believe that I listened to two people who used to eat paste and stick beans up their noses. But I reasoned that they were now young ladies of style and maybe I did need an updated look. Perhaps it was time to get rid of the empire-waisted dresses I still had from the sixties.

Not content to merely put their mother in a black, itchy wiener encasement, they dragged me into the lingerie department to get me some help for my topside. "The dress looks great, Mom," they said, "But your chest needs a little boost." "My chest would need jumper cables to give it a little boost," I answered.

When your go shopping with two grown daughters, you somehow swap roles with them. Suddenly they're in charge and you're the one following after them whining to go home, while they fuss over you and make you try things on that you'd never think of, if you were on your own.

The last thing I ever expected to bring home that day was a pair of foam rubber falsies. My husband saw them lying on the bed and thought I had purchased some toys for the cats.

"Hey, these are great," he shouted as he and the cats played "keep away." "Put those down," I yelled from the bathroom, "You're getting cat hair all over my fake chest." "You're kidding," he laughed, "These things have so much rubber in them, you could bounce off the walls."

"They're supposed to give me that perky, uplifted look. The girls said they looked great."

"The girls also thought the dogs would look great with crew cuts," he reminded me.

He was right, but I had come this far and I was going to go the rest of the way So off I went, taking baby steps because the dress was too tight around my legs. I couldn't really sit, because the black tube was too confining, so we just propped me against the front seat of the car, and I stuck out of the moon roof. Lucky for me it was a nice night.

When we arrived at the party, my husband pulled me out of the car like he was unloading a two by four. I arranged my perky chest, and I let him lead me into the party.

Everyone seemed to be impressed by my dress, and no doubt, by my new figure. It didn't matter that I had no feeling in my body, because beauty is no stranger to pain. I wasn't very mobile, so I spent most of the evening standing by the buffet table, unable to eat. If I had taken a bite of anything, it would have shown up under that dress like a rodent in a snake belly.

After about an hour, the hostess, a sweet young thing with the looks of a goddess and the personality of a dial tone, approached me and said, "You look different."

"Why, thank you," I said demurely.

"No, I mean you look **different**," she repeated and pointed to my chest area. Looking down at my front, I noticed that I indeed did look different. I had one side which Dolly Parton would envy, and one side which looked like Olive Oyl's chest.

Horrified, I realized that somewhere along the line, one of my "fillers" had come loose and had gone AWOL. I gasped, "I know I had two when I came in here!"

Just then, a burst of laughter exploded next to me as another guest pointed to the punchbowl. There, floating like a little island in the sea, drifted my little foam helper, soaking up champagne punch and growing to enormous proportions.

Amidst the hoots and laughter, my dear supportive husband and life of the party announced in a loud voice that I certainly must feel better now that I had gotten that off my chest.

I told the hostess that she could keep it to use as a sponge, and shuffled out as fast as my skinny little dress would let me. On the way out, I bumped up against a wall heater in the hall, and scorched some of my feathers. Passing a mirror in the entry way, I noticed that I looked sort of like a single breasted singed chicken.

My husband was terribly sensitive to my feelings on the way home. He reached over, patted my hand and said, "I'm really sorry that this evening was such a flat bust for you." I saw him smile.

In the course of my lifetime with my family, I have been allowed to leave the house totally unaware that I have a slip hanging down, a strap hanging out, a curler hanging in my hair or a sock stuck to the back of me with static cling. I haven't forgotten these things and I will be avenged. What qoes around comes around and one day I'll be the one to send someone out the door with zippers at half-mast and half price stickers on their backsides. I'll be the one who will "forget" to remind my husband that he still has little pieces of toilet paper stuck to his face left over from his early morning shaving nicks and I'll be the one who won't tell my daughter that she's leaving on a date with spinach in her teeth. Who am I kidding? I won't be the one; I'm too nice.

Laugh 'til the Cows Come Home!

I Have an Hourglass Figure... It's Just That Most of the Sand Has Settled at the Bottom

I have never been thin. When my siblings and I were small, our parents had affectionate names for all of us. My sister was "Twig," my brother; "Slim," and I was "Fluffy." What does that tell you?

When we went shopping for school clothes, we would first visit the "Dainty and Cute" section for my sister. I liked it here because while my mother was busy pulling out size twos for my sister to try on, I amused myself by dismantling and reconstructing the mannequins. I got a kick out of watching people's reactions to a display of children holding their heads in their hands and wearing their feet backwards. I always put them back to normal though, when we left the "Dainty and Cutes" and went into my area, the "Children's Chubettes."

Throughout my young years, I continued to be well padded. Once, when I went to Girl Scout sleep-away camp, we had to give ourselves Indian names for our wilderness walk. My two best friends were "Sings With Birds" and "Dances In The Rain." I chose "Thighs That Thunder."

Later in life, after years of membership to support groups like "Tubs R Us," and still having to lie flat on my back to zip up my jeans, I realized there were several explanations for my condition. First, I decided that I had a chemical imbalance. It was simple; the chemicals in low-fat foods did not successfully balance with the chemicals in my sweet tooth. Candy and deep fried things were a much closer fit. Secondly, and this is scientific, no one has ever really talked about what happens to the weight that people lose. It has to go somewhere, and since everyone around me was always losing it, I concluded that I had some sort of a "fat magnet" in my body that sucked all of those lost weight molecules out of the air and pulled them right to me!

My best friend in college once came up with the brilliant idea that we should spend our spring vacation at a fat farm. I stared at her incredulously. "Why on earth would I want to go to a place where they farm fat? With my luck, they'd want to give me free samples!" I cried.

The only truly comfortable times for me were during my pregnancies. While other normally wand-like girls moaned and sighed over thickened waists and heavier hips, I was in hog heaven.

"Yahoo!" I whooped as I left the doctor's office upon confirmation of my impending motherhood. "Nine months of not having to hold in my stomach and trying to push the excess "me" into industrial strength underwear."

Eventually, however, when I had worn maternity clothes for two years, I had to admit that I had already given birth, and give up wearing those blessed blousy tents. I really tried; my refrigerator was stocked with carrot sticks, celery stalks, skim milk and cottage cheese. I kept them right where I knew I could find them at any time; behind the butter, cream cheese, cinnamon rolls and fudgecicles. I tried to eat yogurt, but I couldn't bring myself to put something in my body that was full of live cultures. I would have felt like I was devouring a little community, and I couldn't bear the guilt of that.

I faithfully played my workout videotape every afternoon; it was full of lively music and fun to watch while I baked brownies. I tried every diet known to the human race, and a few only recognized in the animal kingdom; the Natural Food Diet for instance. On this one, you can only eat nuts, berries and tree bark. After four weeks of that, I felt like a grizzly bear in stretch pants; no thinner, but very grumpy.

I lived by my own diet rules, which were, in my opinion, quite sound in theory. The most basic rule is quite simple; if you eat something in the dark and alone, it doesn't count. The same rule applies if you are A. in a strange city, B. celebrating a holiday, or C. with a friend whose first name starts with a consonant. The calories don't come around under those conditions. It is also advisable to balance out a high caloric food such as chocolate cake, with a diet soda. The soda negates the calories in the cake.

I continued my quest for thindom while wearing loose blouses and expando-pants. My theory of the fat magnet in my body was proven many times over, because heaven knows, I certainly stuck faithfully to my diets. It wasn't hard to do either; it's really amazing how tasty fresh vegetables can be when they are dipped in whipped cream. As a matter of fact, after finishing off a plate, you really don't want any dessert.

The day they had to call the paramedics to unstick me from the turnstile in the grocery store. I decided to break down and join an aerobics class. I was a dues paying member for six months and never lost a pound or an inch. Then my friend Gloria broke the news to me that it's not enough to enroll, even with the best intentions. Apparently you have to go too!

My first day at the class was traumatic. I stood at the back of the room in utter amazement; the place looked like an explosion in a toothpick factory. Twenty-five women, none of whom weighed beyond the double digits, were hopping around in body suits of electric colors and very little cloth. The only fat on any of their bodies was on their earlobes. I was mesmerized by the fact that they were bouncing up and down like hyperactive springs, yet nothing was jiggling.

I began to hyperventilate and my eyes made a quick scan of the room casing it for a snack machine. Just being around these people made my thighs ripple. The instructor bounced up to the front of the room and switched on some music. She was no wider that a sideways dime and wore a teensy little black leotard; she looked like a licorice whip.

Never in my life had I seen so many skinny bodies in one place. This was a class of stick people. Had we all been in a child's drawing, everyone else would have been sketched with a fine tip pen, and I would have been drawn out with a fat marker. I tried to convince myself that my cellulite was merely textured enhancement.

The twig people began bouncing and gyrating to the music, their little wirey bodies twisting like pipe cleaners. Then, all of the sudden, the instructor yelled out "rubber bands!" This sounded to me like a secret code word, but everyone else seemed to understand. I followed the group over to the counter where they each grabbed a long elastic band, with which they did amazing things. They put them over their heads and stretched, they put them between their hands and stretched, and they laid on the floor and put them on their feet and stretched. I was really getting the hang of this, until I stretched too far, lost control and shot that band right out of my hand. I watched in horror as it flew across the room and nailed the Licorice Whip right where her rear end would have been, if she had been large enough to have a rear end.

The next code word was "burn!" This frightened me; I already felt like I had done massive damage to myself with rubber bands. Besides, the word 'burn' has always had a negative connotation to me. I associate it with things like sunBURN, BURNout and first degree BURN. How could this be a good thing? I decided not to take a chance, so I pretended to have a cramp in my leg (I had seen professional athletes do this) and I sneaked to the back of the room to watch my fellow classmates burn.

It was like watching a movie on fast forward. Under the leadership of Licorice Whip, twenty-five women jumped and stretched and burned like they had a leotard full of red ants. Licorice Whip, with her tiny body and her flaming red hair, resembled a matchstick on high speed.

I know when I'm licked and this was one of those times. I was short of breath just watching them, so I took the opportunity to escape into the locker room where I

Adjust Your Attitude

intended to change clothes and make my departure into the real world of real people with real things; things like cellulite, flabby upper arms and saggy bottoms... people with personality!

Something happened to me in that locker room. Pretty soon, the twig-people, who had finished burning, came in, laughing, talking, and perspiring together like members of a sisterhood. Licorice Whip passed by me and said, "It was nice to have you here, and by the way I love your exercise suit." I knew she was just being kind; she probably didn't really love my suit, she just hadn't ever seen one like it, with girdle panels in the front and a ruffle around the bottom to camouflage my thighs. But, she had acknowledged me, and now, in the locker room with the sounds of girl talk and the smell of hairspray, lotion, and deodorant, I felt like a member of the aerobics sorority. As I left the health club, it was with a jaunty spring in my step and a knowing glance toward my fellow health conscious sisters. I walked out onto the sidewalk and thought I caught a glimpse of plump women looking at me with admiration as I strode down the street with my exercise bag over my shoulder. No one ever needed to know that the perspiration on my brow and the flush on my cheeks came from spending fifteen minutes on the floor of the locker room, trying to zip my jeans.

I had taken great strides that day, and as a personal reward, I decided to stride right down the street and into the ice cream parlor...I had worked hard and I deserved it!

Unfortunately, a few months later, the health club burned down, I knew it was bound to happen; anytime you have women "going for the burn" with the gusto of Licorice Whip and company, you're going to have repercussions.

It didn't take me long to fall back into old habits.

"Life is so unfair," I whined to my husband, "I'll never be thin and it's not my fault! I was born with the "F" chromosome."

"What is the "F" chromosome?" asked my nauseatingly thin mate, through a mouthful of chunky chocolate chippity chip ice cream.

"The FAT chromosome," I snapped, "It's very predominant in my family."

"Your mother and sister both wear size 3s," he smugly purred, "and your father and brother could lay side by side on the floor and look like a pair of skis."

"A lot you know," I snarled, "It so happens that it skips around in the generations. When she wore white, my grandmother could have rented out her backside as a moviescreen!"

"You're making excuses," he laughed. This is probably the most annoying thing the man could say to me and he said it often.

"Do you know what your problem is?" I countered, "You have a bad fattitude!" That got him. "A What?"

"A fattitude; a rotten attitude toward fat people. You have the metabolism of a mosquito and about as much body weight. You have no concept of what it is like to have never felt your hipbones."

I think I finally started him thinking. At least he was pensive for a moment and didn't have a snappy comeback. It might have been due to the fact that his teeth were stuck together from the caramel apple he was now gnawing, but I enjoyed the silence.

"What do you need to do is run, like I do." he finally said. Now there was a thought. The last time I remembered breaking out into an all out run was when I chased the school bus down the street trying to catch my daughter who had left home without any underpants. She was seven at the time, and that was long ago. Then, I ran like a cheetah, but my only recent running experience was at the grocery store, trying to get ahead of the person with the piled up shopping cart who was about to enter the express check-out lane.

"I can't imagine running," I stated. "I have never seen a jogger who looked like he was having a good time. Their veins pop out, they are red in the face and they don't smell good."

"It would be good for you," my life's partner continued, "It cleans out your pores, clears your mind, and reduces stress."

"So would a week in the Bahamas," I reasoned.

He was undaunted. "Besides, you will be able to eat anything you want and not gain any weight." With this, he grinned and popped a handful of potato chips into his mouth. Maybe he was right; the man was a virtual eating machine and still weighed about as much as I did on my tenth birthday.

Adjust Your Attitude

That afternoon, he dragged me down to the Runner's Discount Emporium to suit me up. For the novice, purchasing the proper running attire is no piece of cake. There are running shoes, which are not to be confused with walking shoes, which are not the same as exercise shoes, and certainly not akin to sneakers, which were what I wanted to buy.

Then, of course, you have your footwear with arch supports, instep pillows, inflatable soles and power boosters. I finally decided upon the "Generic Gentle Jogger" with metatorsil massage and ankle aerobicizer.

I left the store with the same sense of accomplishment that one must feel after having purchased a precious work of art. These were great shoes; too great to wear with my old sweatsuit. I explained to my husband that if I was to succeed in my new endeavor, it was important for me to feel good about myself. So, I stopped in at the Trendy Trotter and purchased a cute little jogging ensemble in baby blue, with matching sweatbands. I was now the ultimate "accessorized athlete," and felt that I could proudly make an appearance on the jogging trail. Shopping is a wonderful morale booster; I felt invincible.

Bright and early the next morning, my husband popped out of bed as usual, at the ungodly hour of 5:30. "Rise and shine, marathon woman," he chirped.

I wasn't in the mood. "Leave me alone," I mumbled. "Start without me, go wax your hamstring or whatever you runners do."

Mr. Cheerful wouldn't give up. "I thought this was going to be the first day of the rest of your life, and you were going to run straight into it," he cooed.

He said it with such cockiness, I knew I'd never hear the end of it if my feet didn't hit that path. Besides, he was crunching in my ear, and the knowledge that he could eat a candy bar that early in the morning and not gain a millimeter of fat, annoyed me.

I threw back the covers and looked him straight in the eye. "Go over to the park without me," I directed, "And I'll get dressed and be right there. You run farther than I can, so I'll just do the easy course and we'll meet up at the end."

This seemed to satisfy him, so off he went, while I dressed in my spiffy new outfit. Looking in the mirror, I decided that I looked too good to get all sweaty and red faced. My baby blue jogging suit was much too nice to spoil with perspiration, and I certainly didn't want to get my sweatbands wet. Not wishing to bear the ridicule I knew to expect if I didn't follow through with my run, I jumped in my car, drove to the park entrance and ate a doughnut until I saw my beloved, panting and sweaty, approach our designated meeting spot. I dusted the crumbs off my face and reached for the spray bottle of water I had brought with me. With a few quick squirts in the appropriate places, I looked as sweaty as the best of them.

By the time he saw me, I'd had sufficient time to muss my hair and pinch my cheeks for some of that runner's red. "Wow, you beat me, " he gasped, "I really didn't expect to find you here."

"Oh, ye of little faith," I clucked. "All I needed was a little boost, and you, my darling, provided that." I could tell I he was impressed when I described to him the "high" I had felt as I pushed myself to the limit. He was proud, too. So proud, as a matter of fact, that he offered to take me out to breakfast. After all, I deserved it.

And so, at this point in my life, I have come to several realizations. I know that I will never have space between my thighs, I know that my weight number will always exceed my I.Q. number, and I know that God will, no doubt, strike me dead if I ever try to appear in public in a two piece bathing suit.

I no longer believe in three-week diets; the only thing I have ever lost on one of them is twenty-one days. I am aware of the fact that although Jane Fonda, Cher, and Raquel are all close to my age, their sands of time have shifted differently than mine.

On the other hand, I have the satisfaction of having fewer wrinkles than my bony friends, since I naturally puff them out; I am the one that little children want to sit on when it's lap sitting time because I am soft and cushy; and I know that I'm past feeling guilty when I snarf down an ice cream sundae or eat gravy right out of the pan.

As for exercise, I still have my jogging suit and my Generic Gentle Joggers. I wear them while I'm watching my exercise video and baking brownies.

"It's time to go on a diet when the man from Prudential offers you group insurance."–Totie Fields

Spring Cleaning Can Be Frightening to the Domestically Challenged

March has arrived and spring has sprung. Outside, the buds are budding, the leaves that left for the winter are returning, and the world is looking fresh and new. Inside my house, as the early morning sun does its best to shine through the streaks on my windows, I sense that it is time for the inevitable spring-cleaning. I know this because the dust bunnies under my bed have grown so large, they are forming colonies, and there is a science project growing in my refrigerator in the form of a leftover holiday fruitcake.

Every March, I catch the cleaning bug. I survey the collection of winter clutter and resolve to throw it all out, scrub everything down, and begin anew. That powerful drive lasts for about an hour, and then I become overwhelmed with the tasks at hand. I am so overwhelmed, that I do nothing!

It's not that I don't have the desire to clean, it's just that I have never excelled at the art of housekeeping. You might say that I am "domestically challenged." I was raised in the fifties, that pure and simple time when women kept sparkling houses and served tasty, highly nutritional meals, which featured colorful representatives from each of the basic food groups. By all standards, I should have absorbed and embraced the concept of housekeeping.

My mother tried her best to teach me the value of running an orderly household. She was highly organized and efficient in the art of house management. The rule of our house was "a place for everything and everything in its place." I believe she even alphabetized the garbage. All the cans in her pantry were neatly stacked and facing the same direction for easy viewing. I have cans in my cupboard that have been there so long, the labels have peeled off. This has caused a bit of an upset in certain cases, for instance when I served my husband a steaming bowl of "tuna" casserole made with Nifty Kitty cat chow. It was an honest mistake…without the labels, the cans look the same. The interesting result of this is that he now prefers Nifty Kitty to my casserole!

My mother wonders what happened to me. I think she blames herself for the lack of the "neat gene" in my chemical makeup. I understand her dismay, because she is a domestic diva. My mother, bless her heart, could be a poster child for "Dust Bunny Busters." I, on the other hand, keep lint balls as pets.

To others, it may appear that I am not organized…it's just that my brand of organization is not the same as other people's. I have always had my own style. For instance, in the mornings, my family knew to look for their laundry in the oven, where it was drying. It was there because the cat liked to sleep in the clothes dryer and he didn't like to be disturbed before 10 a.m. After so many years of cleaning up after children, I realized that the practical approach was better. I stowed pencils and pens where they would always be handy when the kids needed them to do their homework…in between the seat cushions on the couch, by the T.V. This all made perfect sense to me and I wondered why other housewife/mothers didn't realize the value of my system.

Cooking is another tough one for me. I have always stood in awe of the woman who can take a few eggs, whip them around, throw in some other magic ingredients, and present her admiring guests with a lighter than air soufflé that melts in the mouth. I believe I was the original Cajun cook…everything I tried to fix came out blackened. For some reason, I always had lots of leftovers, so our family had an agreement that anything in the refrigerator that grew a face, or moved under its own power would be thrown out.

Sewing is another art I never mastered. I have never claimed to be a seamstress. I am in awe of the people who can poke a wiggly piece of thread through a microscopic hole in a needle and make pieces of material somehow end up looking like an article of clothing. It's not that I haven't tried, but I quickly realized that my talents lie elsewhere. Clearly, I am not the only one who has ever sewn shut a neckline or put a zipper in sideways instead of vertically. The person who invented Velcro probably suffered from needle frustration, just like me! Because I could not keep my family in "stitches," they grew up being patched with tape and liquid thread. The contents of my mending basket consisted of pins, paper clips, and a stapler. More than once, when a zipper broke, a child of mine left for school stapled into her jumper. My kids always had great posture, because the safety pins that held them together would stick them in their little backs if they slumped.

My daughters are now grown and have families of their own. They cook, they clean, and they sew. If they knew how to do those things all along, why didn't they let me in on it? Obviously, my mother's domestic genes skipped over me and landed in the next generation.

Every Spring, when the world is born anew, I become swept away with the resolve to put my house in order. I march forth with the best intentions, armed with mop, broom, and dust cloth. I swear that I will mend torn clothing, free the closets of anything that hasn't been worn in the past two decades, and rid the refrigerator of plastic bowls containing food remnants of unknown origin. It's scary to find leftovers residing in your fridge, when you don't even recall cooking the meal from whence the leftovers came!

As I embark upon my journey into this year's spring cleaning adventure, I know that this time, I will stick with it. I will conquer the cobwebs in the corner. I will allow nothing to stand in my way of sorting through the sock drawer, discarding the single socks whose mates went into the clothes dryer, never to return. I will pick up the iron that has been serving as a doorstop, and put it to its intended use on the pile of clothes in the laundry room. I will take control of my domestic domain…or maybe I'll go to a movie.

Behold…The Goddess of Romance!

February 14th…Valentine's Day, when some people's thoughts turn to love. I believe in romance, it's just that my life experiences never quite turn out like those of the heroine in a paperback romance novel. I never awaken in the morning with "soft locks of my golden hair cascading carelessly down my shoulders." My hair usually resembles a used cotton swab. No one has ever described my skin as "milky white" or compared my complexion to "peaches and cream"…it's more like granola. I just don't fit into the romantic heroine mold.

Case in point…back in the '70s, I read a best seller which gave fool-proof advice to women about how to capture and captivate a man. I can't recall who wrote it, but whoever it was, clearly lived on a totally different planet than I did. The author suggested that I drape myself in saran wrap and greet my man as he approached the front door after a hard day at the office. I felt a bit skeptical, but who was I to argue with someone as enlightened about relationships as the writer of this handbook obviously was? Valentine's Day was approaching and that seemed like a perfect time to give it a try.

Unfortunately, I found that I had more of me than I had of saran wrap, so I improvised and tied myself into a large garbage bag. Somehow, the desired effect was not there. Undaunted, I topped myself off with a big bow made of twist ties and waited for the sound of my beloved's car in the driveway. When at last I heard him approach, I ran to the front door, threw it open and waited for the excited response that was promised in the book. I got a response all right, but it sounded more alarmed than excited. I often wonder how long it took the poor deliveryman to get over the shock of being attacked by a giant trash bag! Soon after that, I wrapped that romance handbook in the garbage bag and sent it where it belonged…in the garbage.

From that point on, I depended on no one else to instruct me in the ways of romance. I decided that I would rely on my own instincts. I soon learned that my instincts are not reliable. A few years ago, I felt as if my spouse was taking me for granted. I recalled that in the early years of our marriage, I was able to drive him wild when I nibbled on his ear. Now I had more of a chance of driving him crazy when I hid his television remote control. One Valentine's Day, I surprised him with a candlelight dinner for two. When he walked in and saw the candles, he looked at me and said, "Did you forget to pay the light bill again?" So much for the romantic dinner... this would have never happened to the woman in *Wuthering Heights.*

Days later, I planned to spend the afternoon cleaning, so I threw on a tee-shirt and an old pair of shorts. As I walked by the mirror, I caught sight of myself and made the observation that I wasn't in quite as good of shape for wearing shorts as I would have liked. This thought was confirmed a few minutes later, when standing under an open window, I overheard a conversation between my husband and a neighbor. It went something like this:

"What do you think of the legs?" (My husband's voice)

"Well, to tell you the truth, they look like they've seen better days," replied our neighbor.

I heard my husband say, "I know what you mean, and besides, that's a pretty droopy seat." As I stood, stunned by their stinging words, he continued, "I guess that after twenty-five years and two rambunctious kids, there's bound to be some sagging."

That did it! I had heard enough. I knew I was no fashion model, but this was the limit. Who did these guys think they were, talking about my middle aged body like that. I threw open the door and stomped out onto the patio. It was then that I realized that it was not me they were discussing, but my husband's old easy chair that the two of them were attempting to reupholster. When I later told my husband about what I had heard and how I had misunderstood his conversation with the neighbor, he held my hands in his and looked deeply into my eyes as he lovingly said, "Don't be ridiculous...I would NEVER discuss your droopy seat with anyone!" What a sweet talker!

I have come to accept the fact that I am not a heroine in a romance classic. Never in my life have I had suitors lined up at my door like Scarlett O'Hara. Although I have longed to toss my hair, bat my eyelashes and giggle coquettishly, my feeble attempts at flirtation have often been mistaken for muscle spasms. The closest I have ever gotten to being swept off my feet is when I accidentally tripped over the broom when my husband was sweeping off the patio. When some women enter into a room, they invoke appreciative sighs and admiring gazes. Most of the time, when I glide into the den, my husband reminds me not to block his view of the T.V.

We can't all lead romance novel lives. We can't all float on clouds of passion and rapture. Some of us have to stay down on the ground and vacuum. As another Valentine's Day approaches, I sit and ponder the fact that I will never be placed upon a pedestal and admired as a goddess. But the more I think about it, I'm rather glad. Who would want to be worshipped and adored anyway...it would be too much of a responsibility.

Don't Breathe on the Food If It's Not Yours...And Other Rules of Etiquette

One of my earliest childhood memories involves a fancy restaurant and my parents advising me of the inappropriateness of tossing peas into the air. I have another vague recollection of having a maitre d' respectfully request that I not remove the tip money from other diner's tables. These things happened when I was quite young. I now have impeccable dining manners...well, I do slurp my soup occasionally, but I no longer make my chicken drumsticks dance the Can Can on the table.

We all have to learn social graces and that is a task more difficult for some than others. For instance, I have never mastered the art of ordering a dinner that is as tasty as the one ordered by my husband. His is always better. I don't know what it is...it happens every time! I could order a tender breast of chicken smothered in a delicate sauce, accompanied by baby carrots and whipped potatoes that would melt in your mouth. He could order something obnoxious like boiled liver on a stick, and when both orders would arrive...I'd stare at his until he gave it to me. The poor man always has to trade with me. In all the years we've been together, he has never actually consumed anything he originally ordered. The really sad thing is, even after all this time, he seems to be surprised when this happens. He says it's poor manners. I say it's more a case of being "decisionally challenged."

I have a friend who never orders dessert. When that after-dinner tray rolls around, she just holds up her hand and says, "None for me, thanks...I really couldn't." Translated, that means that she is the fastest fork in the west. When the Ultimate Chocolate Suicide Cake, which has been ordered by her dining companion, arrives at the table, she whips that utensil out like a samurai swordsman and has the first piece speared before the plate meets the tablecloth. I have actually felt the breeze generated by the swiftness of her fork. This is guiltless dessert eating. She feels that this way, she can not have her cake…and eat it too. Many would say that this reflects poor etiquette. I say that it is creative dining.

Childhood is a time when we are supposed to learn the basics about table manners. It's good that we have this testing ground of youth on which to experiment and learn what's acceptable behavior and what is not. For some reason, it is not funny when a forty-five-year-old squirts milk out of his nose, although it's okay for a toddler to do the same thing. I don't mind when my two-year-old grandson dips his cookie in my milk and leaves crumbs floating in it, but no full grown, two hundred-pound man better dunk in my glass!

Most people go out to eat at least once a week. Eating is a very social activity and many interesting conversations occur over the dinner table. Some of my most enjoyable dinner companions have been children. They don't stand on ceremony…although sometimes they do stand on their chairs. A while ago, I was speaking to a group of first graders about proper dining manners. I found that they possess some very definite ideas on the subject. I, personally, found their advice to be quite sensible and sound. For instance, how can you argue with this hard and fast rule of etiquette: "When you go out to eat, it's not polite to call the food gross or disgusting. Just take the food, say thank you, and then put it under your napkin when no one is looking. Sometimes you can give it to your little brother if he'll eat it. That way, you don't hurt anybody's feelings." I agree with this concept. It is certainly more preferable than to announce that the food looks and tastes like a science project.

How many times in our lives have we arrived at a dinner, only to be served something that we cannot even pronounce, much less bring ourselves to eat? I remember the time I experienced my first encounter with escargot. I was embarrassed for the hostess who obviously was having a problem with snails invading her kitchen. They had even crawled onto my plate! I would have been much better off, had I known what a little seven-year-old friend of mine knows. His advice is this: "If you go someplace where you gotta wear a tie and some nice clothes, it usually means that the food won't be that fun. You should probably eat something at home first, like macaroni and cheese or something, so you don't waste money at the good restaurant." How true.

I love eating in restaurants. My husband, however, feels more comfortable at home. He says too many forks make him nervous. He doesn't have a phobia of utensils with prongs, it's just that he doesn't like to worry about which one to use at which time. I think he worries too much. I figure that if I don't try to eat peas with a knife, sip wine out of a goblet with a straw, or drink the water in my finger bowl, I'm demonstrating acceptable behavior. I have tried to explain to my husband that he needs to lighten up and follow the three easy steps to dining etiquette as they are described by a young lady of five and a half, "Don't wink at the waiter girls, don't poke anybody else at the table…just keep your hands on your own arms, and don't breathe on food that's not yours…if it's on somebody else's plate or something like that. You can breathe on your own food because they're your own germs anyway."

If you follow those rules, how can you go wrong? Dining out can be a pleasurable experience. It always has been for me…except for the time that I ordered a salad with pepper and the pepper was moving. But that's another story.

I leave you with this, probably the most universal rule of etiquette to be applied in a situation of fine dining, offered by a six-year-old who is wise beyond his years: "When you're out to eat, don't scratch anything…ever! And if you have to burp…DON'T!"

Laugh 'til the Cows Come Home!

Lesson Fifteen: Laughter in Illness and Grief

We live our lives in fear of losing control. When we feel out of control, we lapse into dangerous thought patterns and begin to feel powerless, helpless, and overwhelmed. From this, we often regress into fear and emotional paralysis.

When faced with serious illness or death, our own or that of a loved one, the world tends to take on a different personality. Suddenly, it may not seem so easy to see the positive side of life, much less find anything at which to laugh.

Every person must learn to deal with tragedy in his or her own way. There are no rules. Some people find that laughter is a tool that helps them cope with difficult situations; even serious illness and death. Laughter is not disrespectful; it eases sorrow and allows us to begin the acceptance of the inevitable and the following healing process.

On the following pages, you will find some heart-felt, personal expressions of how laughter has helped some through their times of intense sorrow.

"I Want to Live the Rest of My Life in the Key of Laughter"

I once spoke to a man who was dying. He had been a musician all his life and had spent every day wrapped in the beauty of music; hearing it; loving it; sharing it. As he came to the end of his life, he went through the typical stages of dealing with one's own mortality. He was first in denial, then he was angry, and ultimately found peace with what was happening to his mortal body. And then he began to laugh. When others thought that to be a strange reaction to his impending death, he replied by saying that laughter was music to the soul and he wanted to live the rest of his life in the key of laughter. *Laughter heals.*

Laughter is an important part of the healing process when we have suffered a loss. If you have recently experienced such a loss, this thought might seem inappropriate to you right now. That's okay. This concept is being offered as a collection of people's experiences; people who have used laughter to help them move from grief to another level of acceptance.

It's probably safe to say that most of us feel a little strange about death. We may not fear it; it's just unfamiliar territory. For most of us, it's not hard to identify with Woody Allen's statement: "Death doesn't frighten me. I just don't want to be there when it happens." Baseball legend Leo Durocher had a similar perspective when he said, at age 89, "I don't want to achieve immortality by being inducted into baseball's Hall of Fame. I want to achieve immortality by not dying."

Most of us probably can accept our own death more easily than the death of a loved one. In that case, we're the ones who are being left behind. We weep for ourselves and the memories of the past. When someone near us dies, we are reminded of our own mortality and often, we begin to regret what we never said or did. Our lives become full of "I should have" and "Why didn't I?" I try to take this as a lesson that I should be living my life now, so I don't have those regrets later, but I'm not always successful.

The ability to laugh in the face of adversity is a saving grace and often a link to a sense of stability in an otherwise topsy-turvy, out of control existence. Laughter keeps us connected to the thought that no matter what our condition, we are still living human beings with the ability and the right to feel joy. It allows us to step back and disassociate ourselves from pain and problems so that we may regain perspective. Sometimes, our memory of happy times and our ability to laugh are the only vestiges of the person we used to be. Humor is a link with the past and an affirmation of continuing life and vitality

An individual's sense of humor is a way for him to exercise control over events or conditions that may not be pleasant. A terminally ill woman of 97 expressed this sentiment well, when she told me, "It seems that cancer has eaten up almost every part of my body and the doctors have removed whatever body parts were left. But nothing will ever take away my funny bone because that's what's keeping me sane." *Laughter heals.*

As a whole, society tends to put a certain stigma on dying. By that, I mean there are certain ways we are supposed to deal with it and get through it. Sometimes, behavior patterns exhibited by patients and their families are met with raised eyebrows by others on the outside. For instance, a woman told me that her mother passed away in a nursing center. After their mother was gone, this woman and her twin sister stepped out into the hall. They fully expected to cry, but instead of tears, the giggles came. The sisters began to chuckle and eventually the chuckles erupted into snorts of laughter as they told story after story; reminding each other of the funny things their mother had done during her life.

The flood of laughter acted as a cleansing, healing tonic, but a nurse who had cared for the women's mother came to them and chastised them for their behavior, calling it disrespectful and disgraceful. This caused the sisters to laugh even harder, and in relating the story to me, the woman recalled collapsing against the wall, trying to regain her composure, as the nurse looked on in disgust.

Were the sisters behaving in a disrespectful manner? On the contrary. Their emotions had been at such a fevered pitch for so long, this was the way the "dam broke." In their grief, they needed to remember their mother for the fun and joy with which she had lived her life and raised her children. *Laughter heals.*

A very dear friend of mine handled her untimely death in a most courageous manner. I was, at first, a little taken aback when I received an invitation to her "Going Away Party." It didn't take long for me to appreciate what she was trying to do. Mary needed to celebrate her life with the people who were dear to her. She wanted to "go out" remembering the fun times and the things that made her laugh. As she put it, "I can't change the facts; I'm going to die. But so is everyone else…the only difference is, I know when I'm going. I don't have to look for the pain because it will find me. What I want to do is feel as good as I possibly can for as long as I possibly can, and parties and laughter with my friends make me feel better than anything." *Laughter heals.*

I once had an oncologist tell me that in his treatment of cancer patients, he keeps a constant supply of toys and games in his waiting room. That sounded like a good idea, but I must admit I was rather surprised when he told me that he sometimes wears a clown nose when he greets patients. He explained that our limbic system causes our emotions to be very closely interwoven. According to "Dr. Clown," when many patients come to him, they are frozen with fear. They sometimes haven't yet come to terms with what's happening to them. Seeing the ridiculous clown nose, the ice is broken, and often the nervous laughter gives way to cleansing tears. Walls are broken down and a comfortable patient-doctor relationship is begun. Of course, this doctor was very careful to emphasize the importance of the appropriate use of humor. One must be certain that the recipient of the joke is able to handle it. *Laughter heals.*

The Magic of Laughter

Good humor is like a circle, with no beginning and no end. Positive attitude just feeds on itself and the results are exciting. How old are we when we no longer need laughter? How ill are we when we no longer need to smile? We may not be able to cure ourselves or a loved one, but we can make sure that we know that a person is more than their illness.

Often, people will embrace attitudes that defeat humor. It is important to understand their feelings and rather than attempt to push them into an emotional place for which they may not be ready, we can simply offer them our own positive energy.

Through laughter, we have the wonderful opportunity to provide people with choices. Whether it is us who is ill or a loved one, we can encourage those around us to access joy in adversity. We must all allow ourselves time to grieve, but appreciate that we often find humor in the darkest places. Above all, we must never sit in judgment.

Dr. Bernie Siegel, author of many books on the benefits of positive attitude and humor, emphasizes that only when people fully understand they are mortal, do they start living...in the present. He says, "They can develop the capacity to confront mortality and take on life. People are not living or dying... they are alive or dead; and only when dead, is humor inappropriate."

In working with hospitals and nursing facilities, I have been blessed many times over by the incredible power of the human spirit. I watched in awe as a dying woman let go of this life with a smile and a joke as she laughed in the face of death, saying, "My spirit is leaving now, so you be sure to tell the reverend to remind my family at the funeral that they shouldn't worry about me because this old body is just a shell...the nut is gone!"

I hope I will be so fortunate as to have such a feeling of peace at my death, that I shall be able to "leave 'em laughing."

Lesson Sixteen:
Leaving a Legacy of Laughter

Recently, in assessing my actions for the day, I thought to myself that I had done pretty well. I hadn't grumbled or complained, said anything unkind, acted self-ishly, rudely, or ungratefully, told a lie, lost my temper, or wished for something I didn't have. I hadn't done anything embarrassing or said anything that would support any-one's suspicions that I am sometimes less than 100% confident in my decisions. I was quite proud of myself, so I decided to get out of bed and begin the morning's activities…you see, it was only 7:00 a.m.

That seems to be the way my life goes. No matter how hard I try, I always seem to slip into some bad habits. Sometimes I feel as if the moment my feet hit the ground in the morning, I literally "trip" into the day. I used to beat myself up for that, until I realized that I am a human being with human shortcomings. I will never be perfect, nor will I ever even get close! But what I can do is accept myself for what I am and continue to try to condition myself with the proper attitude in an effort to achieve peace-of-mind and a sense of joy, if not perfection.

Michelangelo was once asked how he could possibly create such beautiful works of art out of lumps of stone. He replied by explaining that he did not create the art; it was already there. All he did was chip away the excess pieces to reveal the beauty that God had created. As participants in life, we are rather like sculptors. The beauty of the human spirit is in us all, but sometimes we need to chip away the excess pieces that cover it up; things like worry, guilt, anger, and negativity.

We are subject to things over which we have no control, but we have a lot to do with how we mold our minds and shape our futures. In everything we do, we are investing in our futures and the future of our world. We become a part of everyone we meet, and they become a part of us. Every one of us is a link in the chain. As friends, parents, children, teachers, and co-workers, we revel in the excitement of our loved ones and support them in the face of disappointment and adversity. That's what connects us all and hopefully, it's the legacy we pass along to our children.

I can't think of a better way to be remembered than to be thought of as a person who liked to laugh. Laughter is the common denominator, which connects all positive thoughts and actions. It conditions our minds and souls and prepares us for dealing with diversity and challenge. Laughter and play allow us to remove ourselves from pain and view our problems from a different perspective.

In working with abused children, many psychologists use puppetry, games, and playacting to reveal a problem and encourage open discussion. Most therapists agree that being able to laugh in the face of a painful situation (not to be confused with using laughter as a mask to avoid dealing with a problem) is the first step in healing.

We all leave our mark in this world and we live on through our children and the people whose lives we have touched. Our names and faces may be forgotten over time, but our lessons and character will always be remembered in the accomplishments of those we have encouraged, loved, supported, and with whom we have laughed.

What legacy are we leaving for the world? Are we living our lives as an example of joy or misery? Are we sending a message that the world is a sad and serious place, full of frustration and agitation? Or are we giving the world the gift of laughter and the knowledge that people may choose peace and pleasure over pain and suffering?

Are we the messengers of doom or are we teaching our children that although troubles will sometimes arise, we have the choice not to be smothered by them? Are we arming future generations with the proper tools to fight negativity or are we leaving them to the wolves?

We are the architects of the future; building gentle spirits and strong minds. If we use the right materials, what we build will last forever. Let our legacy be one of laughter.

Backword

Problems and challenges are part of this life, but they are not the only parts. Nor are they the most important parts. It seems, however, that we always seem to put so much emphasis on the bad stuff, we forget there is another side that needs to be recognized.

Laughter and play are part of the blessings of life and they enable us to grow and live beyond our problems. Positive attitude and humor are integral tools in the areas of pain management, emotional disorders, and physical illness.

These tools allow us to open up discussion on sensitive and difficult issues. Great strides have been taken in helping people of all ages to deal with traumatic events, including abuse, abandonment, addictive behaviors, grief, and more.

In life, laughter is essential in staying focused and helping us to learn, grow, relate, and create. Laughter is a powerful, life-affirming force, which cannot be denied. Lightening up is not a lightweight subject!

Humor is serious business, and hopefully, in this book, you have found a few new tools to help you laugh at the things in your life that have been causing you grief. It is wise to remember that problems are inevitable, but misery is optional. It is possible to add more "smileage" to your life!

Laughter is the thread that winds through the tapestry of life. Personally, I find it comforting to have that thread to hang onto when the rest of my life is unraveling!

If I had my life to live over again, I'd try to make more mistakes next time. I wouldn't be so perfect. I would relax more. I'd limber up. I'd be sillier than I've been on this trip. In fact, I know very few things that I would take so seriously. I'd be crazier. I'd be less hygienic.

I'd take more chances. I'd take more trips. I'd climb more mountains. I'd swim more rivers. I'd go more places I've never been to. I'd eat more ice cream and fewer beans.

I'd have more actual troubles and fewer imaginary ones

You see, I was one of those people who lived prophylactically and sensibly and sanely hour after hour and day after day. Oh, I've had my moments, and if I had to do it over again, I'd travel lighter next time.

If I had it to do all over again, I'd start barefoot earlier in the spring and stay that way later in the fall. I'd ride more merry-go-rounds, I'd watch more sunrises, and I'd play with more children…if I had my life to live over again.
– written by an 85-year-old

About the Author

Drawing upon her experiences as an Educator, Retirement Counselor, Author, and Trainer, as well as a lifetime in the entertainment business, Linda Henley-Smith provides an amusing and educational outlook on working, living and surviving.

A writer, speaker, and performer, Linda has been featured at conventions, conferences, seminars and special events all across the country and in Europe. She is a trainer in high demand and is currently presenting workshops under her company name of "For The Good Times."

With over twenty years experience in teaching and training, Linda enjoys speaking to diverse groups and organizations in the areas of team building, attitude adjustment, stress management and the use of humor in challenging situations. She holds a B.A. and M.A. in Education.

Linda combines her educational background with her affiliations and experiences in business, the retirement industry, health services and the arts in order to bring a wide variety of programs, workshops, seminars and keynotes to all kinds of charitable, educational and business organizations. She implements innovative activities and projects tailored to meet the needs of each audience.

Ms. Henley-Smith's memberships include National Speakers Association, National Education Association, National Marketing Association and Association of Female Executives. She is former editor of Agewave's Senior Magazine and is currently working with schools, medical facilities and corporations around the world, encouraging people to tap into their inner resources in order to achieve maximum success in their personal and professional lives.

Her client list includes organizations such as Wells Fargo Corp., Discover/Novus, U.S. District Court System, American Cancer Society, DeVry Institute of Technology, U.S. West, Farmers Insurance, Humana Health Services, Intergroup, Department of Veterans Affairs and the National Academy of Television Arts and Sciences.

Linda's main focus, which is the motivating and healing power of positive attitude and a healthy sense of humor, has proven to be a popular topic with diverse organizations. The concepts are universal, applicable to all fields and an integral part of the success plan of every individual and organization. Linda is also the author of *"Don't Let Your Fountain Of Youth Get Clogged With the Sands of Time,"* and *"Humor Me ... I'm a Teacher!"*

If you liked the book, you'll love the workshop!

From coast to coast, Linda Henley-Smith's dynamic program has been met with rave reviews. It is a fun, fast-paced, highly interactive presentation which teaches participants to adjust their attitude, learn how to take their work seriously while taking themselves lightly, turn a negative into a positive, and stir up the ashes of burnout to fan the flames of fun.

The program includes:

Incorporating humor into the workplace.
Using humor as a motivator, communicator, and teaching tool.
Maintaining an attitude of altitude.
Utilizing humor as a stress reliever.
Realizing the physical and mental benefits of humor.
Accepting responsibility for your own happiness.
Finding the elf in yoursELF.

Other programs presented include workshops on self-esteem and team building. For more information on programs, products, and books contact:

Linda Henley-Smith
For the Good Times
1 (800) 325-2844

Linda offers the program as a keynote, or as a workshop which can be customized to fit any size group or time frame.

Adjust Your Attitude

Adjust Your Attitude
And
Laugh 'Til The
Cows Come Home!

A Helpful Handbook of Hints
for the Humorally Challenged

By Linda Henley-Smith

To order your copy of:

ADJUST YOUR ATTITUDE AND LAUGH 'TIL THE COWS COME HOME!

by Linda Henley-Smith

MAIL YOUR ORDER TO:

"For the Good Times"
13219 North 8th Avenue
Phoenix, AZ 85029
1-800-325-2844
e-mail: Kitlinda@aol.com

Retail price of each book is $19.95.
All prices in U.S. $

SEND MONEY ORDER, PERSONAL, OR CASHIERS CHECK
(U.S. FUNDS ONLY) PAYABLE TO: Linda Henley-Smith

THANK YOU FOR YOUR ORDER.

--------------------------------✂--

(Please Print Only)

DATE _____ / _____ / _____

_____ BOOKS ORDERED
$19.95 X EACH = _____

SHIPPING & HANDLING $3.00 _____

TOTAL AMOUNT ENCLOSED $ _____

Call For Discounts On Quantity Orders

SHIP TO:

NAME _____ COMPANY _____

ADDRESS _____

CITY _____ STATE _____ ZIP _____

PHONE (___) _____ FAX (___) _____